ThinkTrix
Tools to Teach 7 Essential Thinking Skills

"The Mindful Classroom"

Dr. Frank T. Lyman, Jr.

Kagan Publishing
981 Calle Amanecer
San Clemente, CA 92673
1 (800) 933-2667
www.KaganOnline.com

ISBN: 978-1-933445-31-1

ThinkTrix
Table of Contents
At-a-Glance

Table of Contents

Chapter 1: Introduction ThinkTrix in Action

Chapter 2: Seven Fundamental Types of Thinking the Basic Mind Actions

Table of Contents *(continued)*

Chapter 3: Teacher-Generated ThinkTrix Questions

Chapter 4: Cueing Thinking

Table of Contents *(continued)*

Chapter 5: Activities and Structures for ThinkTrix

Chapter 6: Student-Generated ThinkTrix Questions

Table of Contents (continued)

Chapter 7: ThinkTrix Across the Curriculum

Chapter 8: ThinkTrix Tools

(continued)

Table of Contents *(continued)*

Chapter 8: ThinkTrix Tools *(continued)*

ThinkTrix Glossary of Terms, Bibliography, Appreciations, and A Note to Teachers and Students

Foreword

Foreword
A Letter from the Author

Dear Educators,

This book describes the rationale for using the "ThinkTrix" strategy in the classroom: Regarding "higher-level thinking" in the classroom, consider the proposition that there are at least four possible approaches to oral and written inquiry into content.

First, and most overused is the teacher asking questions and the students responding. At best, this is a Socratic approach; at worst, an inequitable and low-level interchange between a few students and a teacher.

The second, currently in vogue approach is a long list of "prompts," or questions, designed to be similar to test questions. These may have some recognition value on assessment day, but have no metacognitive value and are often inaccessible and/or inane.

The third method, favored by some idealists is to allow most or all questions to come from the students spontaneously. This curiosity-driven, student-ownership strategy may work when the content is relevant, intriguing, or problematic; but requires uninterrupted think time and can exclude many students (leave them behind?).

The fourth, and potentially more effective strategy is one in which students and the teacher craft questions from a basic knowledge of how the mind works. The cueing of fundamental and mutually understood "mind actions" allows for a shared metacognition, every-student-response, higher levels of thinking, and meaningful discourse.

For meaningful, motivating classroom discourse, this fourth way is preferred. I encourage us to try it, along with Wait Time, cooperative interaction, intriguing content, and cognitive mapping.

Sincerely,

Frank T. Lyman, Jr.

Frank T. Lyman, Jr.
Franklyman237@gmail.com

A Letter from Dr. Spencer Kagan

Years ago, Frank Lyman showed me a video of very young children in class as their teacher asked them questions. The teacher cued the children first to think, and then to respond with a kinesthetic hand symbol indicating the kind of thinking the question demanded. The students readily recognized the mind action the question demanded. I was blown away! We all knew the power of metacognition, but here were very early learners doing what high school students would not be able to do without being trained in ThinkTrix. Later, Frank showed me another video in which young children were prompted to generate questions that demanded six different types of mind actions. Again I was amazed to watch. These students knew their minds better than most adults!

In the past few years, I have been researching the brain. It turns out that the six mind actions engaged by ThinkTrix correspond to exercising different parts of the brain. For example, induction (**Example to Idea**) exercises structures in the left hemisphere whereas deduction (**Idea to Example**) exercises structures in the right hemisphere.[1] Similarly, **Recall** engages the hippocampus, whereas **Evaluation** engages specific parts of the prefrontal cortex. Literally, as students practice with ThinkTrix, they are developing their brains!

There is an analogy between what Dr. Lyman has done with ThinkTrix and what my coworkers and I have done with cooperative learning. Many educators think they are doing cooperative learning when they are actually doing unstructured group work. To put students in pairs or teams and tell them to cooperate usually leads to very unequal, unproductive interaction. If we want all students to participate and build off the ideas of each other, we need to structure cooperative interaction. Similarly, to tell students to analyze an historical or literary character calls forth unstructured, usually unproductive mental action. Using ThinkTrix, the teacher might instead structure the mental interaction by saying, think of three or four actions of the character (**Recall**). Next see if you can find something those actions have in common (**Example to Idea**). When you have done that, look for more examples of that characteristic (**Idea to Example**). Finally, give your opinion of the character (**Evaluation**). With structured mental action, with ThinkTrix, students exercise more of their brains and produce a better analysis.

As Frank once told me, *"A river needs banks to flow."* Teams need structure to be productive and so too do minds.

Spencer Kagan

[1] Parsons, L. M., and D. Osherson. 2011. *New Evidence for Distinct Right and Left Brain Systems for Deductive Versus Probabilistic Reasoning.* **Cerebral Cortex**. October. 11: 954–965.

About the Author

Dr. Frank Lyman has been an influential teacher and teacher educator since 1960. Though he is nationally and internationally recognized for educational innovations such as **Think-Pair-Share** and the **ThinkTrix**, he was also an originator of cognitive mapping for elementary students in 1965 in Lexington, Massachusetts. Later coined as **"ThinkLinks,"** this strategy of the visual generation and organization of thinking became standard practice in Maryland as well as nationwide by other names and variations. The recently published book, *The Shaping of Thought: ThinkLinks and Metacognition**, is the product of 45 years of field testing of ThinkLinks in conjunction with its metacognitive partner, the ThinkTrix typology. Dr. Lyman and his colleagues have succeeded in helping students build structures of knowledge and understand their thinking.

In the area of teacher education, Dr. Lyman worked for 26 years with 1,100 student teachers in the University of Maryland/Howard County, Maryland Teacher Education Center. In this setting and in numerous courses and workshops for teachers, his emphasis was on helping teachers learn by experience. He taught that theory is most useful when derived by teachers from their teaching experience, and that those principles derived, become springboards for the discovery of innovative practices. From the synergy with teachers, student teachers, and university colleagues, he has developed theory practice templates including the **"B Wheel,"** and a widely used heuristic called, **"The Problem Solving/Action Research Flowchart."**

Dr. Lyman has degrees from Haverford College, Harvard University, and the University of Maryland at College Park. He has six major awards for achievement in education.

Dedication

I dedicate this book to our son, Frank, a dedicated inventor of ways through educational technology to support students in learning; to Sandra, my wife, the real critical thinker in the household; to our daughter, Sarah, an author who has helped thousands of beginning college students; and to all the teachers who have helped or will help students of all ages solve the mystery of thinking through ThinkTrix.

*****Source:** *The Shaping of Thought: ThinkLinks and Metacognition* by F. Lyman, C. Lopez, and A. Mindus.

Acknowledgments

The ThinkTrix strategy has been developed through planning and implementation by numerous teachers. They took the idea because they were interested in the results with students, and with the students, they multiplied its uses and improved the outcomes. Some of these teachers are mentioned below. Included are teachers who acted as researchers and others who were fascinated with the effects on students. Also deserving mention are the many university and public school educators who encouraged and researched the strategy. They are mentioned in the second section below.

The author would like to acknowledge the contributions of the following educators: Arlene Mindus, Charlene Lopez, Nancy Koza, Shirley Rogers, Teresa Bridger, Thommie DePinto Piercy, Belinda Miller, Tamera Sherr, Sam Polack, Sharon Vargo Olson, Thomas Payne, Hema Kumar, Monica Diaz Palumbo, Kim Flyr, Michelle Zurad, Thomas Cole, Laurie Ann Harvey, Colleen O'Donnell, Kate Thomas, Darlene Sabelhaus, John Krownapple, John Wray, Sorsha Mulroe, Kevin Mulroe, Pat Parrish Wilson, Toni Worsham, Jodi Sacki, Molly Ketterer, Joan Coley, Jeanne Dussault, Sharon Craig, Dianne Hoffman, Janice Knight, Pat Mctighe, Karen Arick, Kathy Glaser, Pat Richardson, Ann Eustis Shad, Ann Mintz, Leah Amato, Anne Swartz, Chips Merkle, Paige McGee, Bill Ferguson, Cathy Orlando, Carla Beachy, Sarah Lyman Kravits, Evelyn English, Karen Foster, Mary Nimmich, Gail Donahue, Barbara Hoffman, Jane Lagioia, Leah Farmer, Barbara Allen, Cliff Bernstein, Barbara Harrison, Mary Ellen Beatty O'Farrell, Larry March, Amy Dower, Carol Phillips, Mary McKnight, Kathy Ryan, Mychael Willon, Nancy Holmwood, Emily Vissers, Betty Disney, Joan Fox, Christine Garrant, Julie Tracy, Carol Dungan, Lisa Singer, Dana Echols, Joanne Durham, Jim Pope, Karen Curtin Atabeck, Carole Eber, Terry Fischer, Margaret Mary Brothman, Rénee Brimfield, Joanne Soporowski, Myra Obaowa, Annette Hart, Tom Bruner, Bev Maddox, Eileen Sanchez, Robert Schwab, Debbie Lewin, Lorna Curran, Sharon Giorgio, Leslie Trinkley, Rebecca Dearman, Gloria Keenan, Kim Miller, Barbara Stuart, Rosalie Gardner, Bonnie Brownell, Nancy Smith, Sally Weidler, Lynne Newsome, Ivin Chan, Francis Baranson, Jane White, Mimi Chiarella, Linda Brown, Bill Gallerizzo, Jody Herman, and Lauri Lee.

University professors and other educators who have been supportive of the development of the ThinkTrix strategy are Joseph Grannis, Richard Arends, Neil Davidson, George Eley, Joyce Murphy, Richard Solomon, Susan Winebrenner, Susan Foster, Evelyn DiTosto, James Raths, Lynda Tredway, Pat Tate, James Greenberg, Pat Richardson, Michael Pressley, John Myers, Jay McTighe, Art Costa, Bill Piercy, Barbara Kapunis, Pat Koskinen, RaeAnn Wuestman, Thomas Brown, Lenore Cohen, June Allred, Ann Davie, Pete Bielski, Wells Foshay, Leo O'Neil, Doris Roettger-Svaboda, Linda Gambrell, Robert Wilson, Wendy Atwell, Virginia Gassner, Kathleen Carroll, Carolyn Adger, Barry Beyer, Alison King, Janet Keeling, Wendy Atwell, Pat Costantino, Jim DeGeorge, Jackie Grabis-Bunker, Lee Smith, Morris McClure, Suzanne Levin, Ellen Miller, Janette Hernandez, Mark Wilkerson, and Doris Novak.

Special appreciation is expressed to Dr. Spencer Kagan for recognizing the transformative power of the ThinkTrix strategy for the cooperative and critical thinking classroom. Spencer and Miguel Kagan were instrumental in the design of the ThinkTrix SmartCard, the wide distribution of which has interested teachers in ThinkTrix nationwide. Appreciation goes to Miguel Kagan and Spencer Kagan for their guidance and review of my manuscript; Becky Herrington and Alex Core for making the book come alive with the design and cover color; Erin Kant for the illustrations; and Ginny Harvey for the copyediting.

The Gist of It!

Classrooms should provide a learning space for all students. Dispelling the mystery of thinking is crucial to providing every student an opportunity to learn. *"How does my mind work to answer this question or solve this problem?"* When students can answer this question effectively, they are able to answer more questions, solve more problems, and inquire more productively. The ThinkTrix strategy creates a shared inquiry and shared knowledge. It is in some sense the Rosetta Stone® of the mind, translating through its specificity the more broadly expressed thinking skills and levels. Once the mystery of how to cognitively proceed is solved, students can more readily join the procession of active learners, able to thrive in the twenty-first century.

ThinkTrix: Tools to Teach 7 Essential Thinking Skills
Kagan Publishing • (800) 933-2667 • www.KaganOnline.com

Introduction

ThinkTrix in Action

Introduction

ThinkTrix in Action

Seven Fundamental Thinking Skills, or Mind Actions, for Schooling and Life
A Metacognitive Approach

Metacognition is defined as knowing how one thinks. It is the mindful act of thinking about thinking, or the conscious awareness of the actions of the mind. Abstract concepts corresponding to mind actions are broad and difficult to comprehend, as they do not readily bring to mind exactly what type of thinking is taking place. The **seven thinking types** of ThinkTrix, properly understood, signify more precisely how the mind is working. All are represented by icons.

 Recall

 Cause and Effect

 Similarity

 Difference

 Idea to Example

 Example to Idea

 Evaluation

In understanding these more fundamental thinking types, teachers and students can achieve a shared metacognition in the classroom. Once these seven types of thinking are fully comprehended, they explain the mind actions involved in more abstract classifications of thinking processes.

Who Is this Book For?

This book is for all teachers K–12. Extensive field testing has shown that the mind actions can be understood and used in first grade and even to some extent in kindergarten. First graders have been taught to use hand signals to show the thinking types. Even sophisticated problem solving is facilitated from second grade up by a working knowledge of the seven thinking types, especially when structured and demonstrated with a charted heuristic, or cognitive path. The value of ThinkTrix for students of all ages, of all performance levels, and in all subjects is demonstrable by the improved quality of their thinking. An accessible metacognitive strategy is the means to the end of higher-level discourse and the insights that result from it.

Sneak Peek
What Does a ThinkTrix Class Look Like?

The teacher asks a question. For Young Students: *"Why did Goldilocks go into the bears' house?"* For Older Students: *"What were some of the reasons the United States fell into the great depression?"* The teacher signals "Think Time" by holding up a fist to symbolize a brain. He or she then holds up both hands to form a T to request students think about the type of question being asked. After 3–5 seconds of Think Time, the teacher gives the "All Share" symbol, and then the whole class responds with a circular motion indicating they understand it is a **Cause and Effect** question. Following that, the teacher has students pair up to generate answers to the question. Knowing the mind action being requested, discussion and answers are more focused.

Students in the class are seated in pairs. Between them is a copy of the Two-Sided ThinkTrix Discussion Board. (See page 145.) The first student places a chip in the intersection of Culture and **Similarity** and formulates a question: *"How is the Indian culture we are studying similar to our own?"* Partner answers. Partner then places a chip in the intersection of **Recall** and Problem/Conflict, asking, *"What were some of the conflicts between the Indians and the Settlers?"* Partner then answers.

A student is reading an essay test question, *"Describe the main character's virtues."* The student thinks, asking herself, which mind actions to use. She decides to use a variety of mind actions: First, she simply recalls some of the actions of the character. She then applies both **Similarity** and **Difference** to describe how those actions are similar to and different from an ideally virtuous character. Concluding, through **Example to Idea** reasoning, the character is often selfish, she applies the **Idea to Example** mind action to look for other examples of selfishness. Finally, she shifts her mind action to **Evaluation** to conclude her essay. Fluent in mind actions, her essay is richer and better organized.

Students are seated in teams. The students are to discuss a science experiment they have just seen. Each team has a ThinkTrix cube or die—each of the six sides is a symbol of a different mind action. A student rolls the die. The die falls with **Idea to Example** face up. The student asks, *"What were examples of using the scientific method in the experiment?"* Using Think-Pair-Square, the students first think about their own answer, then pair up to work with a partner in the team to formulate a fuller answer, and then discuss their answers as a team. The next student then rolls the ThinkTrix die to a different mind action.

What Does One 5th Grade Class Say About ThinkTrix?
Testimonials

"It gets you thinking about what you read."

"You can use it to help you organize your thoughts."

"It helped me in my reading work because it helped me to think up questions. The questions helped me to understand the piece I was reading better."

"It helps you to go more deeply into the discussion than you usually would."

"It helped me to think more specifically and to categorize my thoughts while I am working."

"It helped me to organize my opinions, thoughts, and questions about the book."

"It helps me to think more deeply and gave me a greater understanding of literature."

"It helped me think because instead of allowing my thoughts to run wild, it organized my thinking and helped me to stay on task."

"It is a creative way to metacognate."

"It helped me to focus my thinking into categories, so my thinking was more complete."

"I would explain ThinkTrix in one main word, connections. ThinkTrix help you join connections and ThinkLinks help you find the connections."

"I learned that people actually think a lot about thinking."

"I wrote longer and more thoughtful answers because of ThinkTrix."

"It helped me find the deeper and truer meanings of things that I read."

"I learned that there are many different sides to our own thinking and to other people's thinking."

"I learned that when you think the tangents that you go off on almost always have a certain relation to your original idea."

"It takes up class time by doing much more interesting discussions than you would find anywhere else."

"I believe that both of these methods should be used by those creative teachers and students who fully understand the true brilliance of these inventions."

"It helps me to write better reflections."

"Next year, I can use these types of questions to structure my ideas."

"ThinkTrix helped me think while doing schoolwork because I had the ThinkTrix grid icons stuck in my head, so I thought about each icon and then wrote my answer."

"It will help you generate more ideas, it will help you answer questions with more complete responses."

Source: Shirley Rogers' 5th Grade Class
MOT Charter School, Middletown, Delaware

How to Use this Book

This book can be used as a guide to make classroom thinking more inclusive and productive. Students will learn how they think, learn the value of metacognitive skill, and acquire the knowledge that metacognitive skill can provide. Teachers can use the book as a guide to create a cooperative, engaged classroom that invites meaningful critical-and creative-thinking response from every student.

Student Application of ThinkTrix Mind Actions

There are many ways that students can apply their metacognitive understanding of ThinkTrix mind actions:

- Classify thinking in texts
- Design expository writing
- Classify thinking in journal writing
- Create test questions of varied types
- Classify the thinking in cognitive maps
- Classify and respond to questions in tests
- Create questions for cooperative discussion
- Understand and explain the scientific method
- Write response questions for themselves to answer
- Understand, or translate, teacher questions and prompts
- Identify the steps of problem solving and decision making
- Respond to text by taking notes in various types of thinking
- Use the thinking types as cues to ask questions of colleagues
- Design research, being aware of the steps in problem solving
- Use consciously the thinking types, or mind actions, to respond to any content
- Diagram, or map, any critical-thinking task, classifying the thinking
- Analyze advertisements, political statements, claims, and other exposition

Achievement through Understanding and Using Fundamental Actions of the Mind
The Engaged Student

For students and teacher, a working knowledge of the ThinkTrix typology is useful in six key areas:

1. Verbal communication
2. Reading for information as in written/oral response to fiction and nonfiction, other art forms, and testing
3. Personal and vicarious experience
4. Social, mathematical, and scientific problem solving
5. Inquiry
6. Written composition

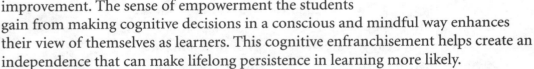

Metacognitive responses in all six areas can be facilitated by the tools and activities described in this book. The main rationale for using ThinkTrix in the classroom is that with an awareness of the basic workings of the mind, students will achieve better and persist in learning more in all six of these key comprehensive skill areas. Student work improves. Metacognitive control of thinking is one cause of the improvement. The sense of empowerment the students gain from making cognitive decisions in a conscious and mindful way enhances their view of themselves as learners. This cognitive enfranchisement helps create an independence that can make lifelong persistence in learning more likely.

There are two necessary components for students to achieve at their highest levels. These are: **active engagement** and **understanding of the task**.

Active engagement is achieved when motivated students have an opportunity to respond and initiate; as enabled by cooperative learning, metacognitive awareness, Wait Time, cognitive mapping, relevant and intriguing tasks and problems, and worthwhile products—the necessary ingredients of an every-student-engaged classroom. Empowered by an understanding of the mind actions of ThinkTrix, students create their own questions and understand how their minds work as they respond. They are prepared to be equal partners in cooperative group work, solve relevant and intriguing problems in structured ways, and gain the sense of independence that builds initiative. To be an effective medium for learning, the curriculum in all content areas and at all levels requires motivated, aware, engaged, and often cooperative response from students.

Understanding of the task, an understanding of the mind actions of ThinkTrix, enables students first to decipher all discourse that requires thinking, oral and written. The teacher builds this understanding by translating all thinking prompts such as inference, analysis, and hypothesis in ThinkTrix language, thereby teaching both the seven thinking types, or mind actions, as well as the higher abstractions that embody them. Educated in this manner, the students are prepared to approach test questions with the question: *"How does my mind have to work to answer this question or solve this problem?"* It is the inability to discern what the question is asking and what type of thinking is required to answer it, that is at the root of many low scores on achievement tests. Understanding of ThinkTrix helps prevent this confusion. For example, students translate test prompts by recognizing that a question is asking for recall, cause and effect, comparison, support for an idea, a generalization from examples, or an evaluation with causes and effects. Having learned how to translate prompts according to what mind actions are required to answer them, the students will answer more accurately and fully. This is demonstrable by comparing test answers written with and without metacognitive understanding. Student understanding of the task is crucial if the student and the teacher are to be able to assess the student's level of knowledge, skill, or understanding, as opposed to simply how well he or she understands the question. Metacognitive awareness through ThinkTrix is an antidote to the often overly abstract and awkward wording of many test questions. If the task is not understood, the student's level of achievement cannot accurately be assessed.

Communication
A Shared Language for Students and Teachers

For any human endeavor, clarity in communication is an essential factor. When understood and used by the teacher and all the students, ThinkTrix mind actions provide a shared metacognition, a common language about thinking. Because the seven types are basic components of more abstract concepts such as inference, metaphor, synthesis, summary, and induction, ThinkTrix renders these higher abstractions more accessible to the minds of teacher and students. This common language not only empowers the students to be more proactive and aware in their problem solving, decision making, inquiring, and creating, it also allows them to better communicate with each other when engaged in these four processes. The "cognitive drift" and "fog," when students hear and use higher abstractions to communicate about thinking, is minimized when a VELCRO®-like connection is made between complex, multifaceted thinking processes and the mind actions of which they are comprised. An example of this crucial connecting, or translating, would be the problem-solving process in which students are asked to "analyze the problem." An abstraction such

Evolution of ThinkTrix

Field testing of **ThinkTrix** began in 1978. Careful examination of hundreds of elementary and middle school students' cognitive maps, or **ThinkLinks**, revealed that seven basic types of thinking later evolved. In some cases, the students had identified the thinking types as **Cause and Effect, Similarity, Example to Idea**, and **Idea to Example**.

The first applied use of these seven types of thinking was the elementary and middle school teachers' wall-cueing of the thinking types and using the cues to remind them to vary the types of questions they were asking students. Teachers were successful and enthusiastic about the cued reminders for making up questions and soon noticed that the students were curious about the seven

(continued)

as "analyze" sets the mind "adrift" unless the precise mind actions necessary to analyze are understood. Is it to be a cause-and-effect analysis, an analysis by analogy, an evaluation of the worthwhileness of the solution effects, or some of all of these?

If students know the seven thinking types, or mind actions, and when to use them, they can respond successfully to the analysis task. If they are not so metacognitively informed, some will still accomplish the task, but many won't. Education is for all students and ThinkTrix will improve the clarity of communication, thereby increasing the percentage of engaged learners.

Classroom Scenarios
Implementation of ThinkTrix At the Primary Level

Nancy Koza, longtime first-grade teacher at Phelps Luck Elementary School in Columbia, Maryland, worked with the question-response cues of ThinkTrix for many years. The following description by Nancy reflects what worked for her. Though it is about her work with first graders, much can be inferred about working with older students.

The introduction of types of thinking begins as early as the second day of school. Initially, all activities revolve around the central theme for the month: **"Teddy Bears."**

Using a large teddy bear, the teacher tells students that they are going to be asked some questions about the bear and that they are to find the answers with their eyes. As questions are posed, students are to **think, share** their ideas with a partner, and then **touch** the answer with their eyes. One or more students are then asked to **touch** the answer with their hands. Examples include, *"What color are the bear's eyes?" "Where is the bear?"* The teacher discusses the similarities between **touching** and **locating** an answer.

If Big Books are used in the classroom, the students continue to **touch** or **locate** the answers to the story questions in both illustrations and text. Once students are comfortable with this process, the **Recall** card is displayed, and the relationship between **recalling** information, **locating** information, and **touching** the answer is discussed. The **Recall** card is now used as a cue for this type of thinking. Not only is the teacher using this cue to indicate the type of question being asked, but also the students are soon able to indicate whether stated questions involve the **Recall** of information.

It is important for students to understand the purpose and significance of this process. Primary students quickly understand that they are better able to answer questions if they understand what type of thinking is being asked of them. They are also made aware that the ability to recognize **Recall** questions assists them in knowing that answers may be stated in illustrations or text and that they may refer back to these sources when in doubt.

Once the students have a clear understanding of **Recall** questions, they are introduced to **Similarity**. Using two teddy bears, the teacher asks students to discuss ways in which the bears are the same. The students discuss their ideas. The teacher introduces the **Venn Diagram** and explains its structure. The **Similarity** card is displayed. The teacher shows the students the lined inner section of the Venn and then records their observations using a red marker.

Using the same bears, the teacher asks students to discuss ways in which the bears are different. The **Difference** card is displayed. The teacher discusses its purpose and symbol, or icon, and records students' observations about the bears' differences using a blue marker.

The teacher then challenges students to identify **Recall**, **Similarity**, and **Difference** questions by asking a question and then having them **type** the question. Methods for pupil responses might include hand signals or pinch cards. This procedure is then applied in all content areas.

The teacher varies the question starters used when posing questions in order to provide experiences with a wide variety of question formats. It is not advisable to post lists of question starters

icons. Teachers then began to teach the meaning and uses of the icons. Students followed by making up their own questions and were thus enabled to recognize the types of thinking in text, tests, and in conversation. At this time, some teachers realized that students could combine the creating of questions with an appropriate cognitive map, or ThinkLink, in which to diagram the answer.

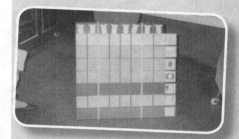

With this step, the thinking types had now returned to the diagrammatic structures from which they originated. Students could make up their own questions, classify their thinking, map their answers, and sometimes write answers using the maps as "blueprints."

At this point in the evolution of the ThinkTrix strategy, a matrix was designed that placed the thinking types on one axis and the departure, or focal, points for the question, on the other axis. (See page 128.) This matrix became in effect, a question generator and

(continued)

Evolution of ThinkTrix
(continued)

discussion catalyst. The matrix was originally conceived as a format for a book discussion between a teacher and a single third-grade student. It soon became evident that the matrix could serve as a tool for discussion between and among several students. The astounding success with the student-to-student interactions led inventive teachers and students in several directions, all of which resulted in meaningful, metacognitive discussion. Belinda Miller designed a two sided matrix that could be viewed the same from opposite sides of the table. It was at the juncture that Tom Payne, coined the term **ThinkTrix**, for thinking matrix.

The next use of the matrix, or ThinkTrix, was to enlarge it as a wall cue to guide question
(continued)

by **type** for student use. When such charts exist, students tend to locate the question framework on the chart rather than analyze the information presented.

It is advisable for students to have firsthand experiences when introducing cause/effect relationships. For example, following a classroom visit by a local beekeeper, the teacher charted students' responses to questions posed in a *"What might happen if…"* or *"if… then…"* format. The teacher assisted students in identifying and labeling the cause and effect components. The **Cause and Effect** card was displayed. The teacher discussed its circular design and encouraged students to expand their thinking by looking for multiple causes or effects in given cause/effect relationships. This understanding greatly enhances each student's ability to explore many alternatives when considering cause/effect situations.

To review the types of thinking presented to date, the teacher places all of the symbols, or icons, on the board and asks students to **type** the questions presented during specific lessons. The teacher stresses the problem-solving aspect of this process.

The most difficult relationship for primary students to understand is **Idea to Example**. This particular type of thinking takes considerable practice. In order to be highly successful, students need to see concrete representations of this thinking. For example, the teacher places six to eight familiar books on the table. The teacher asks students to find the books about bears. The teacher writes this idea on the board and has one student come forward to pick up the appropriate books. The teacher explains that the books this student is holding are examples of the idea, books about bears. The books are then returned to the table. The teacher then states that the next idea is books about friends and writes this idea on the board. The teacher asks a student to find some examples of this idea. After the student selects the appropriate books, the teacher states that these books are examples of the idea, books about friends. Many and varied activities involving modeling and labeling need to be undertaken before students have a clear understanding of this type of thinking.

Perhaps the most effective way to assist primary students with **Example to Idea** is to use **concept attainment**. In this strategy, **Yes** and **No** categories are established. The teacher tells students that all of the items placed in the **Yes** group are examples of the idea, while items in the **No** group do not represent the idea. Exemplars are added to each category. Students observe and analyze these exemplars to formulate an idea.

24 **ThinkTrix: Tools to Teach 7 Essential Thinking Skills**
Kagan Publishing • (800) 933-2667 • www.KaganOnline.com

Once students have had several lessons involving **concept attainment**, the teacher relates this activity to the **Example to Idea** card. The symbols, or icons, on the card are discussed. The teacher continues to provide thinking experiences moving from **Example to Idea**.

Sample Concept Attainment Lesson
Things with Motors

	Yes	No
Car	✓	
Table		✓
Blender	✓	
Vacuum	✓	
Pizza		✓

Evaluative questions deal with the ethical issues of good or bad, right or wrong, as well as other issues concerning value. Students are made aware that the answers to such questions are not generally found in texts but rather require weighing **pros** and **cons**, usually **positive** or **negative** effects. These questions are a natural product of many everyday situations. The teacher introduces the symbol, or icon, for **Evaluation** and discusses with students why a scale is used as a cue. The teacher provides experiences relevant to the students when exploring this **type** of thinking.

Once all the types of thinking have been introduced, the teacher provides each student with a wheel or pinch card and asks students to identify question type during specific activities. The procedure that the teacher might use follows:

- Ask a question.
- Provide **Wait Time** for students to **type** this question.
- Have students indicate their decision on the wheel or pinch card.
- Ask students to **compare** their decisions with those of a partner and discuss the reasons for their choices.
- **Share** the choice with the group and discuss.
- Provide **Wait Time** for students to answer the specific question.
- Ask students to **Pair** and discuss their answers with a friend.
- **Share** the answer(s) with the group as a whole.

As students become more comfortable with the thinking types, they are better able to formulate and type questions of their own. This empowers students to conduct meaningful student-directed discussions in any content area.

Evolution of ThinkTrix
(continued)

formation and classroom discussion. This wall cue even included designations in each cell such as 1a, 1b, 2e, etc. Besides cueing more precisely for the formation of the question, this coding enables students and teacher to quickly refer to the type of question as well as the departure, or focal points, for the question or answer.

The ThinkTrix strategy spread rapidly throughout Howard County, Maryland, elementary and middle schools and then to Carroll County and other Maryland schools. Interest in the enabling tools grew and game boards were designed on which students could land on

a type of thinking or departure point and create questions for a partner or team to classify and respond to. Game board activity spread rapidly in Carroll County where the development of cognitive tools for the ThinkTrix strategy

(continued)

Evolution of ThinkTrix
(continued)

became part of graduate coursework. Throughout this period of discovery, teachers developed and field tested other tools such as large wheels containing the thinking types, small wheels with pointers for individual students, pinch strips with the seven icons, separate movable icons and separate departure points to move in juxtaposition to each other, icons, and departure points on magnets to move on the chalkboards, wheels containing the thinking type

icons and departure/focal points on movable concentric orbits functioning as a circular matrix, problem-solving flowcharts on which the thinking types could be placed, cubes with icons on each surface, and VELCRO® icons.

(continued)

Listed below are just a few of the almost limitless ways that students use this process.

1 Direct students to read a story in pairs. As each pair completes the reading assignment, ask them to look at the cued symbol that has been placed on the board. They are then directed to take turns asking each other this type of question about the reading selection.

2 Before meeting as a group, direct students to read a selection independently, formulate, and **type** five questions related to their reading selection. When the group meets, direct students to review the reading selection by allowing several students to lead a question-answer session based on the student-generated questions.

3 Begin an inquiry project by asking each student to formulate and **type** several questions they might like to ask an **expert** about a new unit of study.

4 After students have completed their original writing, invite them to write and **type** several questions about their stories. During the celebration of their original writing, a student is chosen to read his or her story, and then asks the class to answer the questions he or she has written about the story.

5 Following a discussion in any content area, ask each student to generate one question about the lesson. Record the questions on chart paper. Cut the questions into strips and place them in a paper bag. To review the content at a later date, ask students to take a question out of the bag, **classify/type** it, and then answer it.

26 **ThinkTrix: Tools to Teach 7 Essential Thinking Skills**
Kagan Publishing • (800) 933-2667 • www.KaganOnline.com

It is impossible to establish a firm timeline for the implementation of ThinkTrix in the primary classroom as the rate of presentation varies according to the needs of students. The teacher needs to spend sufficient time on the development of each type of thinking to allow students to have a clear understanding and grasp of the necessary concepts.

Three additional factors have a significant impact on student success. The first is the inclusion of **cooperative learning** strategies in all phases of instruction and implementation. Not only does this provide a means of rehearsing ideas before presenting them to a group, but it also provides peer modeling and assistance for those students who need more practice with various thinking types. The second factor is the **attitude of the teacher as students classify and formulate questions by type**. The teacher needs to provide a supportive, non-critical environment in which the emphasis is placed on encouraging students to discuss their reasons for classifying a question in a particular manner rather than on whether a student's **typing** matches that of the teacher's. The third factor involves the **ownership of ideas**. It is important for each student to realize the value of his or her contributions. As questions are charted in any shape, or form, the contributor needs to be recognized. The teacher accomplishes this by placing the contributor's initials next to each question as it is entered on the chart. When the chart is reviewed, the teacher is then able to identify each student by name as a specific question is discussed. This also provides the teacher with an excellent means of evaluating participation, success in **typing**, and those areas needing further instruction.

All students benefit from participating in this program. This instruction can be implemented in any classroom and provides a powerful tool for students. An understanding of thinking types hopefully reaches far beyond classroom content areas and provides students with valuable tools to use as they seek to understand and solve daily problems they encounter.

Evolution of ThinkTrix
(continued)

Many teachers taught students to label their cognitive maps (ThinkLinks), test prompt writing, and reading response writing according to the types of thinking involved.

Further, to facilitate memory of reference points, teachers used wall charts to list stories, contexts, and concepts in all subjects. Themes of literature, derived by students, were charted on classroom walls. Primary grade teachers had example question starters charted next to the seven icons to help teach and remind. These charts contained a movable mask to prevent overdependence on the starters, thus encouraging metacognition.

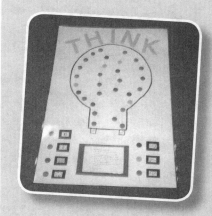

The ThinkTrix strategy and accompanying tools began to appear in curriculum guides throughout Maryland. Numerous videotapes

(continued)

Implementation of ThinkTrix In Elementary Language Arts

were made of elementary students independently and cooperatively generating, responding to, and classifying questions using ThinkTrix. A special-education teacher, Terri Bridger, cowrote a book for teachers featuring ThinkTrix and later wrote a doctoral dissertation on the use of ThinkTrix. Teachers who were experts with various aspects of the strategy attracted teachers from other schools and systems to observe the students at work. One of these teachers, Thommie DePinto Piercy did her doctoral work partly on ThinkTrix. Several journal articles were written by teachers, supervisors, and professors. Workshops were given all around the state. The International Reading Association made a demonstration video of students working cooperatively with the ThinkTrix Discussion Board.

In a remarkable development, a first-grade teacher Nancy Koza developed with the children a set of hand signals to represent

(continued)

In a third-grade classroom, six students are sitting in pairs facing other pairs. On the desks between the pairs are thinking grids, or matrices. The grids are two sided and display seven thinking types and several focal points. Moving among the groups, the teacher listens  to the questions students are asking: *"How is Charlotte like Cricket in* Pinocchio?" *"What caused Wilbur to return to the barn?" "What are some examples of friendship in* Charlotte's Web?*"* As one pair asks the question, it places a marker on the grid to classify the type(s) of thinking involved. In this case, **Similarity** between characters, **Cause and Effect** and event, and **Idea to Example** in the story are the classifications marked. The answering pairs discuss the answer between themselves and agree upon the best answer. *"Charlotte is like Cricket because they both help their friends." "Wilbur returned to the barn because he was scared and he found out pigs can't fly." "Templeton was a friend to Charlotte." "Fern was Wilbur's friend."* All three of the questioning pairs discuss, and in this case agree, with the answers. Then the other pairs converse to decide on their questions by referring to the matrix. The process repeats itself.

In another part of the classroom, individuals are creating webs with ideas in the web center from a wall list of themes from *Charlotte's Web*—Friendship, Helping, Disappointment, Courage, Feeling Terrific. The students choose other titles from a wall list of books and films and link these stories to the idea in the middle by writing them on the strands of the web: "Friendship in *Mr. Popper's Penguins*, in *The Hundred Dresses*, and in *Pinocchio*." Each student is preparing to tell a partner about examples of the theme in each story. They label the webs: **Idea to Example**. Six students are working on the **Cause and Effect** question: *"What are ways a person can help another person change for the better?"* They are working individually using a list of thirty stories on a Wall Chart. Some students are arguing that the question is actually an **Idea to Example** question. The teacher overhears this and agrees that both types of thinking are involved. Individuals choose different stories for examples of helping a character improve. They write the story title and the cause of change on their webs or concentric circle "ThinkLinks." They then look for more causes or the same one in other stories and add these to the diagrams. When the students have found more than one example, they pair up and add to each other's ThinkLink. When class meets tomorrow, they know they are to meet in a group of six and decide which are the most common causes for a person changing for the better. The teacher has told them that they will then have a "theory," or an hypothesis about how people help each other become better people. They will post their hypothesis about common causes, for confirmation through further readings, films, and life experiences.

Implementation of ThinkTrix In Middle School Science

In a Middle School science classroom, students are alternating as they share with partners the ten "weird facts" they have collected from books and the Internet. The assignment was to collect fifty weird facts, or discrepant events, ten in each discipline: geology, astronomy, oceanography, biology, and ecology. The students are discussing each fact or event in any way they want. After each fact is discussed, the pair decides which type of thinking was used in the discussion. To signify their consensus, they move the appropriate icons on the desk to the forefront. **Cause and Effect**, **Similarity**, and **Example to Idea** are the most frequently displayed. To support their decisions, the students revisit their conversations to cite examples of each type of thinking. The teacher moves from pair to pair with interest and humor, listening to the facts and occasionally, doubting their veracity and questioning the sources.

In another section of the room, students are independently designing concentric wheels, in the middle of which they are placing concepts such as adaptation, food chain, erosion, climate change, water cycle, and rock metamorphosis. They are preparing the wheels to contain related weird fact or common facts in the second concentric circle. The outer orbit is designated for other concepts related to each fact. These are called **concept wheels**, and the rest of the class will be invited to add to them at a future time. The thinking is from **Idea to Example** to **Example to Idea**.

Evolution of ThinkTrix
(continued)

the thinking types. The teacher then cued the children to respond to questions by their first giving the hand signal that corresponded to the type of thinking necessary to answer the question. Observing the remarkable level of metacognition displayed by this kinesthetic technique inspired Thommie DePinto Piercy and others to adopt the ThinkTrix strategy.

The most recent stage of the development of ThinkTrix strategy is the practice of the teacher's verbally asking "thinking" questions two ways at once—using the nomenclature of ThinkTrix

along with the more abstract terms. In effect, the teachers are translating questions using

(continued)

Evolution of ThinkTrix
(continued)

ThinkTrix terms. For instance, **hypothesis** is paired with the term **cause** and becomes a **causal hypothesis**; an **analogy** is paired with **Similarity**; a **summary** is translated as a **Recall** of significant events by **Evaluation**; an **inference** is a **causal inference** or perhaps a classification by **Example to Idea** reasoning. Using this translating approach to questioning involves a greater percentage of students in the discussion because they are clear as to what is being asked and how their minds should work to respond. At the same time, students deepen their understanding of terms such as hypothesis analogy, summary, and inference. The cognitive "drift" that occurs when students don't understand how their minds are to work in response to a question is

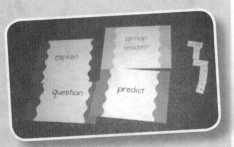

(continued)

A third group of four students is creating a test on the current unit of study, **typing** each question in one or more ways by using the ThinkTrix symbols on the wall. Their assignment includes distributing the test questions as evenly as possible among the seven thinking types.

The last corner of the classroom features four students sitting around a large ThinkTrix science grid. They are making up questions, classifying them on the matrix, answering, and discussing the answers. At the end of the session, they agree upon two questions that will be added to the class quiz.

All students have been asked to design a science experiment containing a **Cause and Effect** hypothesis. The experimental designs will be assembled into a class research booklet to prompt students to carry out experiments or do other research to prove or disprove the hypothesis.

Five minutes before the class period ends, the students reassemble into fixed pairs in which they write independently and share with their partners at least one example of their thinking for the day, including what type or types of thinking were involved. The results of this bridging activity will be shared with a new partner and sometimes with everyone at the beginning of the next day's class. The teacher takes notes on some of these responses and on who made them. Later, some of the responses will be placed on the wall or entered into a retrievable file on the computer.

Implementation of ThinkTrix In High School Social Studies

The High School Social Studies teacher begins the study of the American Civil War with a cascade of facts and opinions. More soldiers died of disease than from warfare; the Civil War was about trade as much as it was about slavery; Baltimore was under federal occupation for the entire war; and so on.

The students have a list of the teacher's statements and are asked to label them true or false. They then choose items that they wish to discuss with a partner. As they discuss the statements, the teacher reminds them to analyze their thinking after each discussion. On the wall in front of the class is the question; *"How did our minds work*

to answer this question or respond to this statement, fact, or idea?" Next to this wall cue are icons for the seven mind actions or, thinking types, of ThinkTrix: **Recall**, **Cause and Effect**, **Similarity**, **Difference**, **Idea to Example**, **Example to Idea**, and **Evaluation**.

Individually, and then with a partner, the students write down the types of thinking they did in the prior pair discussions. They then share the thinking with the class. Analogy, visualizing, cause and effect, doubting, evaluating, and connecting to ideas are some of the responses. The teacher writes these down and demonstrates the importance of metacognition by modeling how to inquire into a fact or opinion by employing multiple mind actions, or thinking types. *"What other wars were similar to the Civil War in respect to death by disease?"* (**Similarity**); *"What caused the high incidence of disease?"* (**Cause and Effect**); *"What were the effects on the war's outcome?"* (**Cause and Effect**); *"From what we can learn about the effects of disease in wartime, what are the general effects of disease on armies?"* (**Example to Idea/Cause and Effect**). The teacher then demonstrates that facts or opinions about a specific event can yield a concept or generalization that can be a focus for inquiry.

To begin the unit of study, the task for the students will be to generate from readings as many facts, opinions, and generalizations, both unusual and common, to serve as springboards for inquiry about the American Civil War and civil war/revolution in general. Textbooks, library books, and the Internet are suggested sources. When the facts, opinions, and generalizations are gathered, students will choose those that interest them, think about and inquire into them using sources and ThinkTrix mind actions, and share their findings with small groups and the class. Accompanying this inquiry will be readings, video, and teacher input on the War. At the end of the study, students will create exams for themselves and others to augment the class exam. Questions on the exams are representative of the seven types of thinking.

Evolution of ThinkTrix
(continued)

partly responsible for several classroom problems, as well as for substandard responses on achievement tests.

The question that this extensive teachers' acceptance and field testing of the ThinkTrix strategy suggests is, *"What would be the effects on student learning and motivation of their having a fundamental understanding of how their minds work when answering a question or solving a problem?"* Said another way, *"What is the educational value of the metacognitive enfranchisement of student thinkers?"* By using the strategies and techniques in this book, as well as some you invent on your own, you can answer this question for yourself. The next steps in ThinkTrix evolution may be yours.

Seven Fundamental Types of Thinking

The Basic Mind Actions

Seven Fundamental Types of Thinking
The Basic Mind Actions

Introduction

The **seven types of thinking** were derived from an examination of hundreds of samples of grade 1–8 students' cognitive maps, or "ThinkLinks," as Maryland students have known these diagrams. Each map consisted of one or more of the seven types of thinking and no others. Despite 30 years of field testing, and some skepticism, these seven have prevailed. Each more abstract term for a thinking skill or process is translatable into one or more of the seven types of thinking, thus rendering terms such as inference, hypothesis, summary, analysis, synthesis, and classification more concrete and understandable. The explanations and examples on the following pages help define the seven mind actions and show their utility.

Recall

Recall is the remembering of experience; literally, putting back together the "members", or elements, of experience. This experience can be personal or vicarious and can include facts, events, rules, people, words, a sequence, an idea, a description, or anything else committed to memory. *"What did he say?"* *"What was her name? Describe what happened." "When did we do that? "What was the formula?"* The mind action of **Recall** is crucial for everything we do and no other action of the mind can be effective without accurate **recalling**, or **remembering**. Conversely, **Recall** often requires another type of thinking in concert. For instance, we can remember a name by association (**Similarity**), or an event by **Cause and Effect** or **Idea to Example** reasoning.

► **Question Starters**
- Who is _____?
- What is _____?
- When did _____?
- How did _____?
- Where did _____?

► **Curriculum Examples**
Examples of **Recall** questions in elementary and secondary curriculum areas could be:

Language Arts
- Where did the story take place?
- Recreate the final scene in *A Tale of Two Cities*.

Mathematics
- Recite the eleven multiplication table.
- What is the formula for the area of a triangle?

Science
- What dinosaurs can you remember?
- What is photosynthesis?

Social Studies
- Who was Squanto and what is he known for?
- What were the key causes, mentioned in class, of the American Revolution?

Art
- Who painted the *Mona Lisa*?
- Who were the most famous Impressionist painters?

Music
- Who were the Beatles?
- What Beethoven symphony can you remember?

Foreign Language
- What is the word for home in Spanish?
- Recite the French poem you learned.

► **Related Thinking Skills**
Memorizing • Remembering

Cause and Effect

Cause and Effect reasoning is the mind action that inquires into the origin and results of an event, fact, or phenomenon. It is an analysis going back to causes or forward to effects. It can be an inference and can lead to a prediction, hypothesis, generalization, or a solution to a problem.

▶ Question Starters
- **Why did that happen?**
- **What, given the circumstances, can you predict?**
- **What causes prejudice?**
- **What are the effects of teasing?**
- **Why do some students achieve more than others?**
- **How can I be become better liked?**
- **How does a person build friendships?**
- **What causes a person not to see the truth?**

Questions like these are asked constantly during the day and throughout life. **Cause and Effect** reasoning is the heart of problem solving, and in fact, survival. All ethical standards and behavior are based on an understanding of consequences, and faulty **Cause and Effect** reasoning can lead to failure in any situation, ethical or otherwise. Scientific thinking depends primarily on **Cause and Effect** analysis, and conceptual frameworks can be built through **Cause and Effect** generalization. Lack of recognition of the importance of focusing specifically on the development of this mind action is a major cause of failed efforts to teach students to solve problems, make decisions, inquire, and invent. People who reason by **Cause and Effect**, and who recognize their own biases, will have more success in day to day living.

► Curriculum Examples

Examples of **Cause and Effect** reasoning in elementary and secondary curriculum areas could be:

Language Arts
- Why did the hero in the story do what he did?
- What are some key ways that authors capture readers' attention on the first page of a story?

Mathematics
- What happens when we keep doubling a number?
- What is the result when a number is multiplied by its reciprocal?

Science
- Explain cause and effect relationships in the food chain.
- What are some effects of gravity?

Social Studies
- Why were some Native Americans upset with the Puritan settlers?
- How could lasting peace among nations be achieved?

Art
- How do you make green from other colors?
- Why have oil paintings lasted hundreds of years without degenerating?

Music
- How do certain kinds of music affect you?
- Why do certain people create music and others do not?

Foreign Language
- How do you learn how to pronounce a foreign language?
- What are the effects of using parallel translation?

► Related Thinking Skills

Hypothesizing • Inferring • Generalizing

Similarity

Similarity is the intersection of like elements. It can be an analogy, a simile, a metaphor, a poetic figure of speech; a comparison of two facts, events, people, narratives, objects, words ideas, and phenomena in which like elements are found.

▶ Question Starters

- **How is he like her?**
- **How do they resemble each other?**
- **How are these two causal explanations alike?**
- **This is to that as what is to what?**
- **How are these two solutions similar?**
- **How are these two problems similar?**
- **Why does this example fit that idea?**
- **What does this remind you of?**
- **How would you feel if someone did the same to you?**
- **What is the intersection of the two sets?**

These questions key the mind action of **Similarity,** but to answer them, some of the other mind actions come into play. Finding **Similarity** is essential to everyday thinking as well as to the construction of knowledge. Concepts are grounded in different examples with similar elements. Events, objects, people, stories, facts, and ideas can be analyzed and categorized by their similarities to other examples in the same general category. False analogies and prejudices are the result of selective reasoning about similarities, as language can be used to create associations that have constructive or destructive consequences. The arts and politics are two domains that make frequent use of **Similarity**. Because of its centrality to human endeavor, the understanding of this intersecting mind action is crucial to success in school and in life, and critical thinking is impossible without it, since matching critical elements is the process by which similarities are found.

▶ Curriculum Examples

Examples of **Similarity** thinking in elementary and secondary curriculum areas could be:

Language Arts

- How are these two stories similar?
- In what ways are the main characters in these two stories alike?

Mathematics

- How is multiplication like addition?
- What does astronomy have to do with mathematics?

Science

- How are tree root systems like river systems?
- What do physics and geometry have in common?

Social Studies
- What were some of the similar reasons that early settlers came to North America?
- What elements do revolutions have in common?

Art

- In what ways are paintings like music?
- Does Cezanne's brush work resemble Monet's? How?

Music
- What orchestral instruments are most alike?
- How is a seventh cord like any thing in our life?

Foreign Language

- In what ways does Spanish remind you of English?
- What metaphors, or idioms, does Spanish have in common with English?

▶ Related Thinking Skills

Comparing • Making Analogies

Difference

Difference entails the finding of unlike elements. It is distinction, or contrast. A difference can be a discrepancy, a nuance, or an inaccurate analogy. It is differentiation, distinguishing.

▶ **Question Starters**
- **How are they different?**
- **What is the different connotation of this word?**
- **Contrast your two favorite sports.**
- **What should I do differently next time?**
- **What are the important differences in cultures?**
- **What distinguishes Earth from Mars?**
- **What do I hope will be different someday?**

The mind action of finding **Difference** is absolutely essential to analysis, problem solving, and decision making. Not all that appears the same is the same, and misjudgments are often the result of mistaken perception of apparent similarities. As noted in the case of **Similarity**, language is often used to deceive by suggesting false likenesses and associations. Finding **Difference** is one of the sharpest tools of critical thinking, and as such, it can function together with the other six to solve problems, make decisions, inquire, and invent/create.

▶ Curriculum Examples

Examples of **Difference** in elementary and secondary curriculum areas could be:

Language Arts
- How are Wilbur and Charlotte different?
- How does free verse differ from iambic pentameter?

Mathematics
- How is the associative property different from the commutative property?
- What distinguishes algebra from calculus?

Science
- How is a mammal different from a reptile?
- Find the discrepancy in that scientific theory.

Social Studies
- How are cities and farms different?
- Contrast two opinions on the main causes of the Civil War.

Art
- How is drawing different from painting?
- What are the distinctions between impressionism and expressionism in painting?

Music
- What are the differences in method between playing horns and playing woodwinds?
- How is jazz different from classical music?

Foreign Language
- How do pronunciation and inflection of Spanish differ from that of English.
- Contrast three different methods for teaching/learning a foreign language.

▶ Related Thinking Skills

Contrasting • Distinguishing • Differentiating

Idea to Example

Idea to Example is the direction of thinking that proceeds from category, concept, or generalization to supporting examples. The reasoning goes from the known to the unknown, beginning with the higher abstraction. With this mind action, thinkers support, substantiate, and categorize.

▶ Question Starters

- **How can you support that opinion?**
- **What examples can you give to substantiate your conclusion?**
- **What are some examples of healthy food?**
- **Defend the rule by showing examples of when the rule holds.**
- **Upon what is your principle based?**
- **Give examples to support that definition.**
- **What makes you think he has that character trait?**
- **That is a generalization. Can you support it with actual cases?**

The ability to confirm an hypothesis, substantiate a contention, support a thesis, develop a concept; in general to discuss by connecting concrete examples to abstract ideas, is essential for successful communication. Aided by a conscious awareness of this tool of the mind, students can avoid the sibling enemies of clarity: vagueness or pointless concreteness. To understand means literally to have examples "standing under" ideas. An idea without an example is a boat without a rudder; it goes into a sort of cognitive drift and loses its power to communicate what is intended. The closest mind action is **Similarity**, as examples of a concept or generalization have elements in common.

Questions such as those above are essential if discourse is to be rational and if conceptual knowledge is to develop. Much incivility in societies is marked by unsubstantiated assertions and associations, often in the form of emotive sound bites. No concept or generalization can be understood unless anchored to multiple examples. The task for teachers is to delay defining until students have the concrete foundation for the concept (avoiding the "rush to rubric"). The task for critical readers/thinkers is to be wary of unsupported ideas as well as examples that are force fitted to ideas.

► Curriculum Examples

Examples of **Idea to Example** thinking in elementary and secondary curriculum areas could be:

Language Arts
- What are some examples of friendship in books?
- What are some examples of cross-cultural heroism in literature and real life?

Mathematics
- Circle the even numbers.
- Give examples of probability.

Science
- Name some dinosaurs.
- Defend that hypothesis.

Social Studies
- In Westward Expansion, name some of the groups of people who went West.
- Give examples of Southern complaints about U.S. government tariffs before the Civil War.

Art
- Show some examples of the use of light in paintings.
- Show some examples of impressionism.

Music
- Raise your hand when you hear a crescendo.
- Raise your hand when you hear a piece by Mozart.

Foreign Language
- Raise your card when you hear the best accent.
- Make a web to show all the words you can that have the same root.

► Related Thinking Skills

Categorizing • Deducing • Substantiating

Example to Idea

Example to Idea is the direction of thinking that proceeds from the given example or examples to a concept or generalization. The reasoning is from the known concrete to the unknown higher abstraction. With this mind action, thinkers conceptualize, generalize, classify, induce, and discover.

▶ Question Starters

- **What is the concept common to these examples?**
- **From these events, what general statement can you make?**
- **How would you classify that behavior?**
- **What is your hypothesis given these data?**
- **From all this information, what do you conclude?**
- **What is the main idea here, and what examples support it?**
- **What do you make of what just happened?**

The ability to hypothesize, generalize, conceptualize, and classify is at the heart of knowledge construction, transfer of knowledge, and scientific thinking. It is the empirical path, championed from Aristotle to John Dewey to Jerome Bruner. Knowledge that moves us forward is developed through curiosity and necessity. These twin drivers spark the question, and the question moves the mind from example(s) to idea and sometimes on to confirming example(s). To make the best use of the concrete to abstract mind action in the above questions, students need to be aware that their experiences and biases influence the ideas they derive. Otherwise, experience becomes the willing or unwitting tool of opinion and worldview. Self-aware concept attainment, discovery, and generalization are essential for raising the educational level of all students.

Though an **Example to Idea** question or statement is easily identified as such, the thinking required to respond may bring into play several mind actions; in the case of multiple examples to idea, the **Similarity** action, especially.

► Curriculum Examples

Examples of **Example to Idea** thinking in elementary and secondary curriculum areas could be:

Language Arts

- What are some character traits of Pinocchio when he is a puppet?
- What is the most important idea, or theme, in *Romeo and Juliet*?

Mathematics

- In this set of numbers, what comes next?
- From these examples, create a rule for finding the area of a triangle.

Science

- What do you notice that all these animals have in common?
- From these experiments, what hypothesis can you derive?

Social Studies

- Why do you think these three cities were built where they are?
- From the description of these conflicts, how would you classify them?

Art

- These three sculptures are all examples of what?
- What do you notice about this painting, and how would you classify what you notice?

Music

- What does this music make you want to do?
- What mood does this music evoke?

Foreign Language

- These three words are all related. How?
- Knowing the root of this word, what do you think it means?

► Related Thinking Skills

Classifying • Inducing • Generalizing

Evaluation

Evaluation for the purposes of the ThinkTrix typology is the weighing of the value of an event, a fact, an enterprise, a work of art, a phenomenon, or an idea. It encompasses the ethical dimension, as well as the rating or ranking of the worthwhileness of any experience. It is not synonymous with all meanings of *"judgment."* All **Evaluation** requires judgment, but not all judgment requires **Evaluation**; as in, *"In my judgment this example does not fit in that category."* This statement requires **Idea to Example** thinking.

▶ Question Starters
- **Should I do this or not? Why?**
- **What is always wrong?**
- **What is the most important thing I did?**
- **What does it take to be considered a nice person?**
- **How should a government support the social contract?**
- **What is the ethical decision that should be made?**

Evaluation is crucial for problem solving, decision making, and prioritizing. In some cases, it requires the weighing of consequences, and in ethically complicated situations, the consequences are judged on the basis of their effects on living things and valued objects. In these situations and in others requiring the weighing of options, **Cause and Effect** reasoning is always a component of **Evaluation**. The other mind actions can also come into play in certain situations.

▶ Curriculum Examples

Examples of **Evaluation** questions in elementary and secondary curriculum areas could be:

Language Arts
- Did you like the book? In what ways?
- Was Ahab right to pursue *Moby Dick*? Why or why not?

Mathematics
- How does math help us in life?
- What type of equation works best here?

Science
- How should we act to preserve nature?
- Which is the better way to do this experiment?

Social Studies
- What are some of the ways that the Puritans treated the Native Americans? Evaluate these acts.
- What are the benefits and costs of having a democracy?

Art
- What painting do you like best? Why?
- To what extent were Picasso's influences on art good or bad in your opinion?

Music
- What is your favorite music? Why?
- Do you prefer pop music over rock? Why or why not?

Foreign Language
- Which language sounds better than English? How?
- In what ways is English a useful language for the world?

▶ Related Thinking Skills

Decision Making • Judging • Prioritizing • Valuing

The Continuum within Each Thinking Type: The Third Dimension

It is important for the teacher to understand that within each thinking type there is a **continuum of complexity**. For example, within **Cause and Effect** some questions may ask for a simple cause or effect and others may elicit a complex generalization. An example of the simple **Cause and Effect** question would be *"Why did this chair move?"* and a complex question would be *"What causes prejudice?."* This latter question would engage the mind to inquire into multiple examples using **Example to Idea** and **Similarity** thinking types; the former would require a single observation. In introducing the thinking types, it is not important to show this extra dimension of ThinkTrix. It will gradually become clear as students ask, identify, and answer questions in class. The teacher can eventually make clear to the students that some questions within each type require more thinking than others, and even require adding more types to answer the question. This can be demonstrated by multiple examples.

The following is a continuum within each thinking type and gives an explanation of the "third dimension" of ThinkTrix as a metacognitive tool. For many years, teachers have attempted to expand students' thinking into levels beyond **Recall**. Taxonomies of complex levels of thinking have been designed and incorporated into virtually all universities' education departments. The use of these taxonomies in actual classrooms has proven to be difficult at best. Teacher's text editions have been better at meeting the various levels but students are rarely "let in" on the level of thinking at which they are being asked to work. This section explains a system of symbols that function as cues for various types of thinking. The symbols are prominently displayed in the classroom and used on many classroom devices (cognitive tools). Each symbol represents a continuum of thinking. This section explains this "third dimension" of ThinkTrix—the continuum within each type.

The symbols are:

Following is a continuum for each thinking type:

Recall:

| details, | facts, | events, | sequencing, | summarizing |

Concrete/Simple ←————————————————————→ Abstract/Complex

Cause and Effect:

| visible/explicit | inference, | prediction, | hypothesis, | generalization |

Concrete/Simple ←————————————————————→ Abstract/Complex

Similarity/Difference:

| objects, | events, | systems, | personalities, | stories, | ideas, | theories |

Concrete/Simple ←————————————————————→ Abstract/Complex

Idea to Example:

Example for class of object, fact, or event   Example for class of idea, generalization, or theory

Concrete/Simple ←————————————————————→ Abstract/Complex

Example to Idea:

event, person, object, or system
to one or more ideas

event(s), person(s), object(s)
or systems to one or more
most important ideas

events, persons, objects, or systems
to one or more common ideas

Simple ←————————————————————→ Complex

Evaluation:

| objects | decisions | personalities | ideas |
| events | systems | works of art | theories |

Concrete/Simple ←————————————————————→ Abstract/Complex

Following are examples of questions in each of the areas. All questions refer to *The Wizard of Oz*. It can be assumed that virtually all readers will be familiar with this selection.

Recall :

1. What did the scarecrow's hat look like? (detail)
2. What was the name of Dorothy's dog? (fact)
3. What happened after the tornado picked up the house? (event in sequence)
4. Briefly summarize *The Wizard of Oz*. (summary)

Cause and Effect :

1. What made Dorothy and her friends fall asleep? (visible, explicit)
2. Why was Dorothy on her way to see the Wizard? (character motivation, explicit)
3. Why was Mrs. Gulch so angry at the world in general and Dorothy in particular? (emotional, implicit)
4. What do you think Dorothy will do after she says, "There is no place like home."? (prediction)
5. What might have happened if the house had landed on the Mayor of Munchkinland? (prediction about a hypothetical situation)
6. What do you think Dorothy will do the next time Toto is threatened? (prediction about a hypothetical situation)
7. What do people do when their friends are threatened? (generalization-theory making)
8. What causes people to feel threatened? (generalization-theory making)

When a teacher, with the students using the **Example to Idea** and the **Evaluation** mind actions, asked third graders to discuss in pairs what the most important idea in *The Wizard of Oz* is, two girls decided that it is "There are some things in life you don't realize." The teacher decided at that moment that there are some things about ThinkTrix that he had not realized.

Similarity/Difference:

In the **Similarity** and **Difference** categories, the questions themselves are easy to develop and are often stated broadly. It is the answers that are more or less concrete or abstract. Therefore, following each question below, there are examples of possible answers beginning with the concrete and moving up the ladder toward the abstract. Of course, the questions asked could be geared to the level of answer desired, *"What common character traits do…?"*

    1. In what ways are Dorothy and the Scarecrow similar?

      Possible answers:
- They both have eyes, feet, and ears. (very concrete)
- They both are in Oz. (concrete)
- They both need a favor from the wizard. (a little more abstract)
- They both prove to themselves that they have talents they didn't know they had. (more abstract)
- They are both empathetic and caring individuals. For instance, Dorothy wants to save her dog and all the people she meets, and the Scarecrow risks his life to help Dorothy. (abstract)
- They both represent feelings of inadequacy, which are in all of us, and thus help to show us that we can accomplish what we set out to do. (highly abstract)

Idea to Example:

1. Who were some of the Munchkins? (concrete)
2. What are some examples of unusual creatures in *The Wizard of Oz*? (less concrete)
3. What are some examples of magical powers in the Land of Oz? (more abstract)
4. What are some examples of evil, meanness, friendship, caring, empathy, frustration, or revenge in *The Wizard of Oz*? (abstract)
5. What are some examples of friendship in literature? (abstract and complex)
6. What are some examples of symbolism in *The Wizard of Oz*? (highly abstract)
7. What are some examples of symbolism in literature? (highly abstract and complex)

Example to Idea:

1. What are some of Dorothy's feelings? (simple inference or classification)
2. What are some of the ideas that come to your mind when the friends are approaching the Great Oz? What are their feelings? (more complex inference or classification)
3. What are some of Dorothy's character traits? Tell what examples you used. (complex inference or classification)
4. The Scarecrow's brain, the Tin Man's heart, and the Lion's courage are all examples of what idea? (complex analogy)
5. Dorothy saving Toto; the Lion, Scarecrow, and Tin Man helping Dorothy, and the Good Witch giving Dorothy ruby slippers; are examples of what emotion or feeling? (complex analogy)
6. The Wizard's attempt to leave at the end as well as Dorothy's enthusiasm when she wakes up are examples of what central theme? (highly complex analogy)
7. What are some of the morals or lessons in *The Wizard of Oz*? (This question forces one to look at all the events in the story, make generalizations of lessons learned, and convert them to recommendations for society). (highly complex inference and generalization)
8. What is, for you, the most important idea, or theme in *The Wizard of Oz*? Why? (This question forces critical thinking, or evaluation, requiring complex weighing and comparing of alternatives. As is the case with other highly abstract and complex questions, this question requires the mind to journey through several other thinking types.). (highly complex evaluation)
9. What is the most important idea in life? (*the* question)

Evaluation:

Evaluation questions may be more or less abstract, more or less complex, and more or less significant with regard to importance or impact. The following questions exemplify this continuum. Also each question is followed by why, which requires **Cause and Effect** thinking.

1. Was it right for Dorothy to dance as she went to see the Wizard? Why? (low importance)
2. Was it right for Dorothy to run away from home? Why? (more important)
3. Was it right for Dorothy to melt the Wicked Witch? Why? (higher importance)
4. Was it right for the Wizard to knowingly send Dorothy back into a dangerous, life-threatening situation for her to get the Witch's broom? Why? (high importance)
5. Was it right for the Wizard to pretend to be great and powerful? (complex, abstract, important)
6. Should people ever pretend to be what they are not? Why or why not? (highly complex, abstract, important)

Introducing ThinkTrix to Students
Cracking the Code

There are at least three effective ways to introduce the seven mind actions to students. These can be used separately or in some combination.

One method is for the teacher to post the seven icons in the classroom and refer to them as "the code of the mind" that students should try to "crack." The teacher then proceeds to craft questions, referring the students to the relevant icon(s) after the question is asked. Eventually, through this variety of the concept attainment/inductive strategy, the students begin to understand the type of thinking symbolized by the icon. To extend this inductive reasoning, the teacher can ask the students who have "cracked' the meaning of an icon to keep their opinion a secret. When the majority of students think they have the answer, the teacher can reveal it. At this point, the teacher and students can begin crafting questions using the given icon and checking for understanding among themselves.

Another approach, slightly less motivating, but effective, is for the teacher to use direct concept-attainment lessons for each thinking type. This would entail, for instance, asking or writing several **Cause and Effect** questions under the "yes" column and asking what they have in common. Other types can be placed in the "no" column. Once sufficient numbers of students have individually or cooperatively come up with the **Cause and Effect** concept, students can create their own questions of this type and have the teacher or other students verify the questions as requiring **Cause and Effect** thinking. This procedure can be repeated for each of the thinking types over time until the meaning of each of the icons is clear.

A third approach to building the shared metacognition with the class is for the teacher to first pose problems, dilemmas, and novel facts/situations/phenomena. The students then ponder these motivating starters and write down how their minds are working as they think individually and discuss in pairs. As they report on their thinking, the teacher can create the seven thinking type icons from their "whole cloth." With this approach, the students gain a sense of ownership of the ThinkTrix mind actions.

They will understand that the seven thinking types are simply a representation of the thinking they do every day and not something esoteric or not useful. The results of this activity remind the teacher of a similar truth—the ThinkTrix strategy is not an "add on," but rather a way to make conscious, and thereby more useful as a tool, that which has been automatic and unconscious.

The teaching of the use of the thinking matrix with its focal, or departure, points follows the development of an understanding of the thinking types/mind actions. The teacher can do this easily by modeling the crafting of questions at the intersecting cells on the matrix. The students then practice using the double-sided ThinkTrix to create questions and discuss how their questions fit the cell. Then, cooperatively, they proceed to answer the questions. When meaningful discussions follow, the true importance of shared metacognition is revealed.

Throughout the teaching of the meaning of the icons it is useful to use visual organizers, or ThinkLinks, such as webs, wheels, Venn diagrams, flowcharts, and dangling boxes to give visual representations of the mind at work. **ThinkLinks** is a student-friendly name for the cognitive maps, named by Tom Bruner, and is used commonly in Maryland. In this way, the students "see" their thinking, thereby developing a deeper understanding of the mind actions. Later, when they create their own thought "shapes," they will know more readily and indicate what types of thinking are contained in these visual organizers. Another way to speed up and deepen metacognitive understanding early on in the process is for the teacher to introduce hand signals to represent each thinking type. This kinesthetic approach has the potential to "seal" the understanding, especially when students use the hand signals themselves.

Teacher-Generated ThinkTrix Questions

Teacher-Generated ThinkTrix Questions

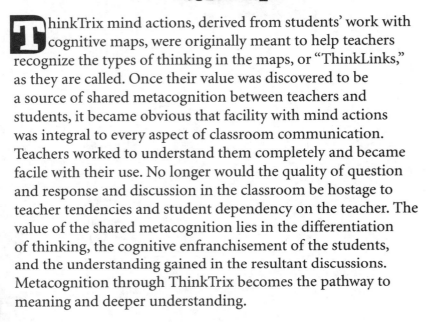

Rationale

ThinkTrix mind actions, derived from students' work with cognitive maps, were originally meant to help teachers recognize the types of thinking in the maps, or "ThinkLinks," as they are called. Once their value was discovered to be a source of shared metacognition between teachers and students, it became obvious that facility with mind actions was integral to every aspect of classroom communication. Teachers worked to understand them completely and became facile with their use. No longer would the quality of question and response and discussion in the classroom be hostage to teacher tendencies and student dependency on the teacher. The value of the shared metacognition lies in the differentiation of thinking, the cognitive enfranchisement of the students, and the understanding gained in the resultant discussions. Metacognition through ThinkTrix becomes the pathway to meaning and deeper understanding.

ThinkTrix was induced originally from student work on cognitive maps, or ThinkLinks, and was assumed to be merely an interesting insight. The fact that teachers can have difficulty in the press of the moment to think of questions at various levels of complexity, led the discovery team to realize that the thinking types, now mind actions, could be employed as wall cues to help the teacher think of more complex questions on the spot.

Visual cueing devices that catch attention and ensure that teacher memory and student response are enhanced. The fact is that within the complex classroom situation, no amount of planning can ensure that teachers can always remember to do what they know is best. The visual cueing devices below are some of those used successfully by teachers and students as reminders to engage the full range of mind actions.

A wide variety of visuals serve as aides as teachers generate questions:

▶ **Separate icons on magnetized cards**—The teacher manipulates the cards, moving them to prominence individually or together. The pairing of icons allows the student not only to see which mind action prompted the question, but also which ones are required to answer it. See pages 156–169 for blacklines.

▶ **Separate icons on cards (Thinking Types Posters)**—Each mind action can be on a separate card and permanently placed visible to the entire class. The teacher generates questions by referring to the cards, eventually encouraging the students to do the same. See pages 156–169 for blacklines.

▶ **Mind Actions Wheel**—This wheel with the seven mind actions can be placed on the board or wall with tape or magnets, or even hung around the teacher's neck. The teacher points an arrow or arrows toward the type(s) of thinking in play at the moment. It can be miniaturized to a Handheld Thinking Wheel for small group interaction or every-student-response. See page 171 for blackline.

▶ **WheelTrix**—This tool is a circular version of a matrix. When the teacher asks a question, both the corresponding thinking type and the focal point, being on separate moving orbits, can be aligned with each other at an arrow point. It could be hung around the teacher's neck as well as placed on the wall or the board. See pages 172–174 for blacklines.

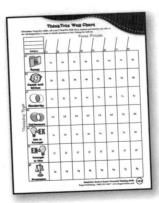

▶ **ThinkTrix Wall Chart**—This is a large wall-chart-sized matrix with the seven mind actions in the rows, and the points of departure, or content specific focal points, as the columns. Each cell of the matrix is designated by a number and a letter to enable quick mutual recognition of the cell. The teacher uses this large chart to generate questions, enabling the teacher and eventually the students to maximally differentiate the classroom thinking. See page 177 for blackline.

▶ **Random Question Generators**—These tools are Spinner Wheels and ThinkTrix Cube Die or Dice. The teacher spins the pointer arrow and asks a question requiring thinking of the designated type. The die can be rolled with the same effect. These tools and all the others can be accessed and manipulated by the students. Sometimes they are miniaturized for this purpose. See pages 170–175 for blacklines.

▶ **Question Starter Chart**—This chart provides multiple question starters under each thinking type icon and word. The chart is helpful to the teacher at the early stages of the learning process, but once teacher and students are facile with the mind actions, the Chart or Sample Question Cards should be taken down or covered. Dependence on these models interferes with metacognitive awareness. In general, they are more useful in the early grades. See page 66 for blackline.

▶ **Transactional Signals and ThinkTrix Mind Action Cues**—Each mind action can have a corresponding hand signal, or sign. The teacher can either give the signal(s) for a type or types of thinking or ask the students to signal the type(s) of thinking on cue after Wait Time. This kinesthetic every-student-response technique is instructive and motivating at all grade and performance levels. It can be used also among students in cooperative groups. The signaling is appropriate for a question being asked or for a response given. See pages 77–78 for charts.

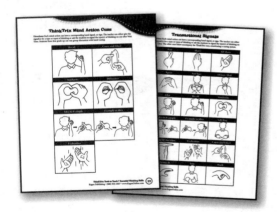

Primary Models for Teaching The Mind Actions

Used in Primary Grades to Develop Mind Action Concepts

Recall: The observation and retrieval of facts, plot design, sequence, detail, and summary

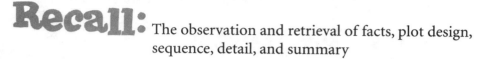

❓ Question Starters

- Who is _____?
- How did _____?
- How many _____?
- Where did _____?
- What did _____?
- What is _____?
- When did _____?
- Which is _____?

❓ Question Examples

- Who was chasing the Gingerbread Boy?
- How did Dorothy find Oz?
- How many children are in Ramona's family?
- Where did Cowardly Clyde live?
- What did Henny Penny tell each animal he met?
- What is a washtub?
- When did the Three Bears see Goldilocks?
- Which happened first: (event) or (event)?
- Where did *Charlie and the Chocolate Factory* take place?

❓ Write Your Own Questions

1. _____
_____

2. _____
_____

3. _____
_____

Primary Models for Teaching The Mind Actions
Used in Primary Grades to Develop Mind Action Concepts

Cause and Effect:

Cause, effect/result, motive, consequence, inference, prediction, and hypothesis

? Question Starters

- What caused (or causes) _____?
- What are the effects of _____?
- Why did _____?
- Why do you think _____?
- What would have happened if _____?
- How did _____ affect _____?
- (Statement) Why?
- If _____, then _____.
- What influence/impact did _____?

? Question Examples

- What caused Cinderella's unhappiness?
- What were the effects of being indoors in the story *Trouble in the Ark*?
- Why did Amelia Bedelia do such unusual things?
- Why do you think Noisy Nora came back home?
- What would have happened if all the animals had stayed in the farmer's bed in *One Cold Wet Night*?
- How did the strange voice affect the old lady in *My Big Toe*?
- Fern's parents did not like her talking to animals. Why?
- If the wolf had blown down the third little pig's house, what would the pigs have done?

? Write Your Own Questions

1. _____

_____

2. _____

_____

3. _____

_____

Primary Models for Teaching The Mind Actions
Used in Primary Grades to Develop Mind Action Concepts

Similarity: Analogy, ratio, comparison, intersection, and common element

? Question Starters

- How are _____ and _____ alike?
- How was _____ the same as (like) _____?
- What is the same about _____ and _____?
- Compare _____ and _____.
- Name _____ who (that) is similar to _____.
- _____ and _____ are alike in what ways?
- _____ is to _____ as _____ is to _____.
- Who is similar to _____?
- What is like _____?

? Question Examples

- How are Brown Bear and Hairy Bear alike?
- How was the setting in *Cowardly Clyde* like the setting in *Sleeping Beauty*?
- What is the same about _____ and Mary in *Mary Had a Little Lamb*?
- Compare the problem in *Lucy Didn't Listen* to the problem in *Pinocchio*.
- Name another character in another book who is similar to Ira in *Ira Sleeps Over*.
- *The Gingerbread Boy* and *Pinocchio* are alike in what ways?
- The Fairy Godmother is to Cinderella as Wendy is to _____.
- What other character is like Pinnochio?
- What character are you most like? How?

? Write Your Own Questions

1. _____

_____

2. _____

_____

3. _____

_____

Primary Models for Teaching The Mind Actions
Used in Primary Grades to Develop Mind Action Concepts

Difference:
Distinction, discrimination, and differentiation

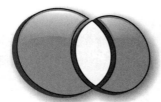

Question Starters

- What are the differences between _____ and _____?
- How is _____ different from _____?
- What distinguishes _____ from _____?
- Contrast _____ and _____.
- Why is _____ not like _____?
- What's different about _____?

Question Examples

- What are some of the differences between Amelia Bedelia and Mrs. Wishy-Washy?
- How is Lamb in *Who Will Be My Mother?* different from the little girl in *Grandpa, Grandpa?*

Write Your Own Questions

1. _____

_____

2. _____

_____

3. _____

_____

Primary Models for Teaching The Mind Actions

Used in Primary Grades to Develop Mind Action Concepts

Idea to Example:

Categorization, deduction, substantiation, analogy, and support

? Question Starters

- What are some examples of _____?
- Find some examples of _____.
- Give an example of _____.
- What kinds of _____?
- List the types of _____?
- Name some _____.

? Question Examples

- What are some examples of kindness in *Cinderella*?
- From our list of favorite stories, find some examples of fantasy.
- Give some examples of misunderstandings in *Amelia Bedelia*.
- Give an example of a time when someone you know acted like the elves in *The Elves and the Shoemaker*.
- Name some story characters who are thoughtful of others.

? Write Your Own Questions

1. _____

_____

2. _____

_____

3. _____

_____

Primary Models for Teaching The Mind Actions

Used in Primary Grades to Develop Mind Action Concepts

Example to Idea:

Classification, induction, conclusion, and generalization

Question Starters

- What kind of person was _____?
- What is the main idea of _____?
- _____ is an example of _____.
- What word best describes _____?
- What is your hypothesis?
- _____ and _____ are examples of _____.
- What type of _____ is _____?

Question Examples

- What kind of person was Rapunzel?
- What is a moral of *The Little Red Hen*?
- *The Lion and The Mouse* is an example of what type of literature?
- A beautiful dress, a pair of glass slippers, and a handsome coach are all _____.
- What word best describes Amelia Bedelia?
- Minnie likes to hang by her hands, hang by her knees, and jump on the bed. What does this tell you about Minnie?

Write Your Own Questions

1. _____
   _____

2. _____
   _____

3. _____
   _____

ThinkTrix: Tools to Teach 7 Essential Thinking Skills
Kagan Publishing • (800) 933-2667 • www.KaganOnline.com

Primary Models for Teaching The Mind Actions

Used in Primary Grades to Develop Mind Action Concepts

Evaluation: Value, judgment, rating, weighing evidence, and prioritizing

? Question Starters

- Do you think it was (good, bad, right, wrong) for _____?

- What was the most important _____? Why?

- How would you rank _____?

- If you had your choice, would you choose _____ or _____?

- Should _____ _____?

- Do you agree or disagree with _____? Why?

- Would you rather _____? Why?

- Do you like _____? Why?

- Were they right or wrong to do that? _____ Why?

? Question Examples

- Do you think it was right for the animals to go back into the mud after Mrs. Wishy-Washy had given them a bath?

- Was it right for Pinocchio to run away?

- Do you think that the Gingerbread Boy was brave or foolish? How?

- Who do you think was the hero in *Charlotte's Web*? How?

- What do you think Cowardly Clyde should have done after he saw the ogre?

- If you had your choice, would you pick Ira or Mary Jo for a friend? Why?

- Should Ira have asked his friend about the teddy bear? Why?

- I think that all children like the story of Cinderella. Do you agree?

- Would you rather read a mystery story or an adventure book? Why?

- Is reading important? Why?

? Write Your Own Questions

1. _____

_____

2. _____

_____

3. _____

_____

Using the Matrix
How to Use ThinkTrix to Generate Questions

- **Getting Ready.** Copy the ThinkTrix blackline below. Fill in the Subject (e.g., Language Arts, Math, Art). Fill in the Focus Areas for the subject (see ideas below the matrix).
- **To Generate Thinking Questions.** Each cell in the matrix suggests new thinking questions. When first learning, use the Question Starters on the right side of the matrix to help come up with questions. Teachers can generate questions on the fly to ask students in class during discussion, create a list of questions for future student interaction, or create test or essay questions.
- **Interaction in Pairs or Teams.** Using the matrix, one student on the pair or team generates a thinking question and poses the question to his or her partner or team. After Think and Discussion Time, the next student generates the next question to discuss. Students may ask each other to identify the type(s) of thinking required.

Subject _____

ThinkTrix   Focus Areas

Type of Thinking						Question Starters
Recall						• Who is ___? • How did ___? • What is ___? • Where did ___? • When did ___?
Cause and Effect						• What caused (or causes) ___? • What are the effects of ___? • What would happen if ___? • What influence/impact did ___? • If ___, then___?
Similarity						• How are ___ and ___ alike? • What similarities do ___ and ___ share? • Compare ___ and ___. • ___ is to ___ as ___ is to ___. • What is like ___?
Difference						• What is the difference between ___ and ___? • What distinguishes ___ from ___? • Contrast ___ and ___. • Why is ___ not like ___? • What's different about ___?
Idea to Example						• What are some examples of ___? • Give an example of ___. • Support your idea. • List the types of ___. • What kinds of ___?
Example to Idea						• What is the main idea of ___? • What word best describes ___? • What is your hypothesis? • ___ and ___ are examples of ___. • What type of ___ is ___?
Evaluation						• Do you agree or disagree with ___? Why? • What was the most important ___? Why? • How would you rank ___? Why? • Were they right or wrong to do that? Why? • Do you like ___ ? Why?

Focus Area Ideas for Each Subject

Here are possible Focus Areas to fill in for the vertical axis on the matrix for each subject
- **Language Arts.** Reading, Writing, Vocabulary, Grammar, Spelling, Style, Imagery
- **Literature.** Setting, Plot/Event, Character, Feeling, Point of View, Conflict/Problem, Relationship, Moral/Theme, Trait
- **Mathematics.** Number, Set, Operation, Algorithm, Property, Concept/Rule/Axiom/Theorem, Problem, Application
- **Science.** Person, Object, Animal/Plant, Environment, Process, Experiment, Concept//Principle, System, Hypothesis
- **Social Studies.** People/Groups/Organizations, Place, Time/Change, Power/Governance, Global Connections, Culture, Event, Concept, Generalization, Historical Perspective

ThinkTrix
Mind Action Charts

Mind Action Charts are used at all levels to remind students of the meaning of the mind actions. The charts are not generally openly displayed after their initial role as reminders.

Recall	Cause and Effect	Similarity
• Facts • Plot design • Sequence • Detail • Summary • Visualizing	• Cause • Effect/Result • Motive • Consequence • Inference • Prediction • Hypothesis	• Analogy • Ratio • Comparison • Intersection • Common Element
Difference	**Idea(s) to Example(s)**	**Example(s) to Idea(s)**
• Contrast • Comparison • Distinction • Discrimination • Differentiation	• Categorization • Deduction • Substantiation • Analogy • Support	• Classification • Induction • Conclusion • Generalization • Finding Essence
Evaluation		
• Ethical Consideration • Judgment • Rating • Weighing Evidence		

Recall	• Tell the sequence of events in *The Ransom of Red Chief.*
Cause and Effect	• What are the effects of teasing? • What do you think causes a rainbow? • What would happen if the earth rotated only once a year? • Why was Ahab wrong to push after Moby Dick?
Similarity	• How are the causes of the Revolutionary War and the Civil War similar? • What feelings does Pinocchio have that Wilbur also has? • How is Johnny Dorset like Tom Sawyer?
Difference	• How is a rhombus different from a parallelogram? • How is a mammal different from a reptile?
Idea to Example	• What are some examples of irony in *The Ransom of Red Chief?* • From our list of stories, find some examples of friendship. • Show some examples of the distributive property.
Example to Idea	• What are some character traits of Dorothy? • What are the themes of *The Karate Kid?* • From the evidence, what conclusion do you draw? • From these examples make up a rule for use of quotation marks.
Evaluation	• Was Ahab right or wrong to push on after the whale? • What is, for you, the main idea of *The Wizard of Oz?*

ThinkTrix Mind Actions as Translators For Critical Thinking and Discussion

In classroom discussion, teachers can achieve shared metacognition and clarity by asking students questions posed in two distinct ways, one way after the other. The teacher first asks the question using the common, more abstract vocabulary; and then asks it again using the more concrete language of ThinkTrix mind actions. The second, more concrete way clarifies the first, more abstract way. This "translating" enables all students to understand. The examples below illustrate this clarifying process.

Common Questions

Mind Actions

1. **Of what does this remind me? How is it similar to something else I know?**

2. **With what does this contrast? How is it different from what I know?**

3. **Why did this happen? What caused this?**

4. **What are the consequences? What are the effects of this?**

5. **What evidence supports this? What examples fit this idea?**

6. **How valid are these assumptions? Are these ideas based on real examples?**

7. **How would I classify this? What is the best idea to fit this example?**

8. **What assumptions underlie this? What idea is behind these examples or ideas?**

Common Questions	Mind Actions

9. How would I summarize this? What are the key ideas here?

10. What is the thesis, or main idea, that represents the examples in this passage?

11. Is this ethical, or right? How should I evaluate this? What are the positive and negative effects of this?

12. Do I believe what is being said here? How is the writer trying to persuade me? What counter argument could I make, or what different conclusion or idea is possible? Is this true? How does the writer know? Do the examples fit the ideas? Are the ideas supported by real examples? How could I find out?

13. What point of view, or perspective, is guiding these statements? What is the underlying idea that influences these ideas and examples?

14. What inference can you make? What is the possible cause of this?

ThinkTrix Flashcards
Teacher Sample
Designed by Todd Marrone

Teachers and even students can create their own icon cards of any size. Students can be artistic as they take ownership of the mind actions in artistic form. The cards below by a teacher and professional artist can be used as an enticing model for students who wish to create their own cue cards.

Todd Marrone was an Art and gifted teacher for 16 years at Welsh Valley Middle School (Lower Merion School District) in Narberth, Pennsylvania. He was also a phenomenal artist who died tragically at a young age. These ThinkTrix Flashcards were designed by Todd and are shown with permission from his wife, Heather Hall.

"A thing does not end nor begin with the maker. Things are consumed, produced, and consumed again within an aesthetic ecosystem. I nudge my work, encourage it, steer it, but I don't make it from scratch nor do I individually own it. It doesn't just create a dialogue, it is a dialogue. I am a participant in the conversation. A thread in the tapestry. A rung in the ladder."
—Todd Marrone

http://toddmarrone.com/makers-statement/#sthash.LFIH5Dvu.dpuf

Implementation of ThinkTrix in Test Construction

The framing of questions is not a simple matter if students are to be given a fair chance to understand what is being asked. In classroom discourse, the teacher can translate every thinking prompt with language that is keyed to the seven thinking types. However, test-question writing demands that attention be paid to the question framing. There is no chance to translate for students during the test, though they can be taught to do the translating using ThinkTrix. This problem of lack of clarity—the over abstractness, poor syntax, and even irrelevance of some test questions, is the cause of some of the low test scores. The following deconstruction and reconstruction of test prompts on a state third grade practice test demonstrates this problem and how knowledge of ThinkTrix can inform test-prompt writing and student understanding of the prompt. The prompts below are critiqued by examining the wording, the difficulty in understanding the question as written, and a way to better word it using ThinkTrix as a guide.

Prompt. Think about the deserts and what they are like. Give one reason why people might choose to live in a desert community.

How the Mind Works. *"Think about deserts."* [Picture in your mind]

"What are they like?" [Prompt appears to be calling for ◯◯. *"What would you find in a desert?"* requires 💡**EX** and 📁 thinking.]

"Give one reason why people might choose to live…". [This question asks the mind to comprehend what positive effects would cause a person to want to live there. 🔄 and ⚖️]

Prompt Revision Using Precise Language. Think about the deserts.* Picture them in your mind. Picture in your mind what you would have to do or what would happen to you if you lived in a desert community. *"What would cause a person to want to live there?"* Give one reason.

*The expression, "Think about…," when left open should translate to the student as visualizing. The expression, "Give a reason," means a good or bad cause or effect.

Prompt. In the United States today, a large number of people are moving to communities in states such as Arizona, Nevada, and Utah, where there are large areas of desert. List two things that could happen to the desert environment as more people move there.

(continued)

How the Mind Works. "List two things... could happen to"* is language for effect [🔄 and 💡-EX].

The students should understand the question to be asking, "people moving to the desert could cause what two effects on the desert environment?"

*Things do not happen! Things are objects!

Prompt. What information about traveling in the desert could someone learn by reading, *Crossing the Sahara?*

The skill is supposed to be summarizing, but the children in no way are cued to summarize. Summarize means to bring forward the most essential ideas or examples. [💡-EX, EX-💡, 📁].

How the Mind Works. Students should see this as a recall-visualizing exercise and free associate images to write down.

When this prompt calls for "text-based ideas," they are not always ideas! They are in some cases examples or facts. If we want ideas, we have to ask for them. In other words, if the prompt requires summarizing, it should be clearly asked for.

Prompt Revision Using Precise Language. Think about and picture in your mind the traveling in the desert you read about in *"Crossing the Sahara."* Now write everything you remember. [📁 , 💡-EX].

Prompt. Explain why Geoffrey Moorhouse's trip might have been a good experience for him. Use information from what you read when you answer.

How the Mind Works. [📁 , 🔄 , ⚖️]. The question requires the student to recall the trip, to consider the effects of events on Geoffrey Moorhouse, and to select the good, or positive effects (nowhere does it show signs of being related to "Compare Ideas" as suggested in the scorer's notes).

The words "good", "bad", "right", "wrong" indicate evaluation and should also signal effects and weighing the effects. [⚖️ , 🔄].

Also, if the questioner wants more than one answer he or she should say so. You get what you expect, except from high-initiative learners. Can it be that sometimes this is a test of initiative as much as anything else?

Prompt. Use the information from the passage to write a paragraph about one of the major events during Geoffrey Moorhouse's trip.

How the Mind Works. Recall. Again, this requires visualizing the event. "To write about" is a **Recall** [🗂] prompt when open like this and requires visualizing. The best response is a recreating of the event either in first or third person. Why not ask for this?

The prompt doesn't ask the reader specifically to do either. Also, "major" is unnecessarily obscure for third graders. What about "important." Is this a vocabulary test or a thinking test?

Prompt. Use the information from this passage to tell why you think Geoffrey Moorhouse selected a Tuareg for a guide.

"Use the information" is a **Recall** prompt, and "why," in this case, calls for **Cause and Effect** response. "You think" cues the child that there may be a difference of opinion. Again, only a child with initiative or serious practice will put more than one answer. Why not write the prompt "What do you think are some of the reasons that Geoffrey Moorhouse selected a Tuareg?" A metacognitive translation of the question is, "Geoffrey Moorhouse wanted a Tuareg for a guide. What do you think he thought would be some good effects of this Tuareg's guiding"; or, "What do you think caused Geoffrey Moorhouse to want a Tuareg to be his guide?" [🔄]. The question also requires **Evaluation** [⚖].

Prompt. Put an X next to the reading passage that gave you more information about desert life. Again, the vocabulary test and the adult syntax. Why not say… "told you more" about desert life or at least use this phrase next to "gave you… information". Metacognitively, the passage (Why not say "story part" to third graders?), is most accessible (decodable) to children when they use the **Difference** mind action. It is also a case of **Idea to Example** thinking. "More" and "less" are cues for contrast, or **Difference** [💡EX , 🔵🔵].

Prompt. Write a note to your teacher explaining why the passage you selected gave you more information about desert life… WOW! "Write a note" has a specific connotation for 8-year olds and not the one meant here. "passage you selected…" Why not write "story you chose told you more"? Most serious, however, is the use of "why" in this prompt. "Why" is generally a **Cause and Effect** indicator. It could be translated nonsensically from the question as written "what caused the passage to give you more info…?" At least "how", or "in what way", would be more appropriate since what is really being asked

(continued)

here is how the example fits the idea [💡EX]. **Difference** thinking is also involved. At best, reword the question to read "Write a paragraph (since "paragraph" is being used everywhere else) to your teacher giving examples of how one story tells more about desert life than the other story." We don't want a test to be a reflection on adult imprecision in language and lack of knowledge about children's vocabulary level (their testing situation vocabulary level in particular).

Prompt. Look at the last picture… How does it show Tuaregs using the environment to meet their needs? "Look at" cues the visual which helps **Recall**. "how does it show" is an indicator for **Idea to Example** thinking. The reader is looking for needs-meeting examples in this case.

The phrase "using… environment… needs" works despite curly cues, since children hear this all the time in school, though nowhere else. Would it be more accessible to word the question "Give examples of how the pictures show Tuaregs using… needs"? Again the expectation of multiple answers is not made clear in the prompt.

Prompt. How are your needs and wants the same as or different from those of the Tuaregs in the desert? "Same and different" are cues for finding **Similarity** and **Difference**. "Needs and wants" are social studies concepts that confuse third graders almost as much as do flawed explanations of fact and opinion. Wouldn't "needs" do it here? Have "wants" been stressed in the "passage"?

Prompt. How are the lives of the people described in the readings different from those of people living in the deserts of the U.S. today…? [📁 , ⬭ , 💡EX].

Is this an answerable question for third graders? How do they know anything about how people live in the U.S. desert today? Do they mean Phoenix? Is that a desert? Death Valley? Also note the shift from "passages" to "readings". Not only does the vocabulary shift, but both terms are inaccessibly abstract, or metaphorical, for 8-year olds. This happened earlier, though less seriously, with the shift from "choose" to "select" when "want" would be more universally understood.

The examples above were taken from a teachers' workshop examining a state test sample. These comments show how ThinkTrix-facilitated metacognition can aid in writing and understanding/interpreting test prompts or any questions. From the commentary, it can be inferred that the teacher and student will benefit from knowing the mind actions of ThinkTrix by applying them to reduce the cognitive fog that obstructs the path to a true assessment of knowledge. Action research has shown this to be the case.

Cueing Thinking

Cueing Thinking

The swirl of activity in the classroom requires that all participants, including at times the teacher, be cued to respond. The systems of cueing must be mutually understood and when appropriate, prominently placed.

Transactional cues between and among teacher and students facilitate metacognitive recognition and use of the thinking types/mind actions, as well as the meaningful conversation that flows from this recognition. Every classroom dynamic is rendered more effective and engaged by the use of agreed upon cues for response and transitions.

Teacher and Student Hand Signals

Teachers can use a set of agreed upon sign language signals to cue the mind actions required to answer or create a question. Also, students can ask the questions and give the signals. For example, the student or teacher asks the question and the responders, after appropriate Wait Time, hand signal the type(s) of thinking they will use to answer the question. Another variety is that teacher or student can show the signal and the responders can make up a question of that type. Besides the obvious metacognitive value of this kinesthetic mode of cueing, it acts as a translator for the higher abstraction thinking terms such as hypothesis, summary, inference, assumption, and prediction, and main idea. By pairing the more abstract term with its component parts mind actions, the questioner clarifies both the higher abstraction and further develops the concept of the mind actions. The teacher can do this translating by asking the question two ways; for example: *"What is your hypothesis? I mean by that, what is the cause of the event?"* However, hand signaling the mind action focuses students sometimes more effectively.

This kinesthetic, or oral technique, of translating through metacognitive cueing is effective in grades 1–12. No technique has been shown to be more effective in helping students gain an understanding of how their minds work. The conversations that follow the questioning are the proof of this contention.

ThinkTrix Mind Action Cues

Directions: Each mind action can have a corresponding hand signal, or sign. The teacher can either give the signal(s) for a type or types of thinking or ask the students to signal the type(s) of thinking on cue after Wait Time. Students from first grade up can run group discussion with hand cueing.

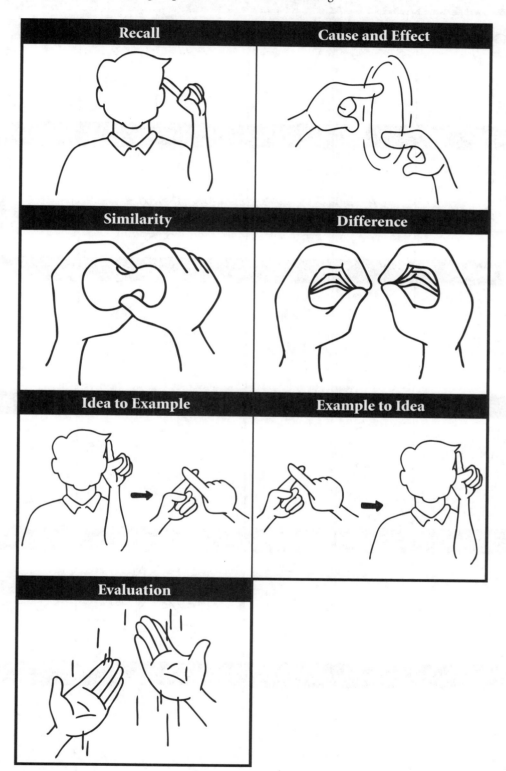

Transactional Signals

Directions: Each mind action can have a corresponding hand signal, or sign. The teacher can either give the signal(s) for a type or types of thinking or ask the students to signal the type(s) of thinking on cue after Wait Time. The other cues below accompany the ThinkTrix cues, constituting a cueing system.

Think	Pair	Share	All Share
Disagree	Agree	Not Sure	I Know That
In My Mind	Idea	Recall	Similarity
Difference	Idea to Example	Example to Idea	Self Hug
Good Risk Taking	Type of Question	Evaluation	Cause and Effect
Thought Connection	Picture It	Vote	Work

Visual Cues

In addition to hand signals, teachers use a variety of visuals to cue thinking. Teachers can point to the desired mind action on a poster, or have students dial a wheel to the mind action the teacher wants students to engage. Arming the various visual cues are cue cards, wheels, matrices and charts, cubes and dice, as well instructional technology.

► **Cue Cards**—Teachers and students use a variety of question-response cue cards to indicate understanding of thinking types and to prompt meaningful discourse. Examples of card cueing are a set of icons on cards for every student, as a strip, or on separate cards. With cue cards, teachers and students can prompt questions, or identify the mind actions within questions and in texts or on tests. The cards can be used with the whole class or within cooperative groups. The seven types can be matched up with departure points, also on cards, to classify or create questions. For this matching, and in fact for discourse of any kind to have "flow" in the classroom, a wall cued list of books, concepts, or contexts is necessary. Memory must be facilitated. Also, large cards can be magnetized and manipulated on the blackboard. This affords the teacher the opportunity to do some silent signaling for discussion as well as for written response.

► **Wheels**—Each student can use a wheel with a pointer, displaying all seven mind actions. On cue, students can set their wheels to identify types of thinking during discussion or while reading text. Some wheels can have two pointers to show that. This wheeling is particularly useful and motivating within cooperative groups. When students are cued to display their wheels after moving the pointer, the teacher can check for understanding and even ask the students to justify their classification to a partner. Some wheels can have moving concentric orbits with thinking types in the inner orbit and focal points in a second orbit. This is in effect a matrix in motion and can be used with contexts, wall cued ideas, and ThinkLink shapes to craft, answer, and show responses to complex questions. A large wheel of either of the above kinds can be positioned on the wall or blackboard or even hung around the teacher's neck. Wheels are popular with students. As in all activities with the ThinkTrix strategy, the value lies in the meaningful conversations and writing that follows the metacognitive recognition of the thinking.

▶ **Matrices and Charts**—A large ThinkTrix matrix on the wall or a chart rack is useful for focusing the class, thereby allowing the teacher and students to easily create questions. Allied with the ThinkTrix chart should be a chart containing the contexts of the classroom curriculum as well as wall cued cognitive map (ThinkLink) shapes. The cells of the matrix can be designated with numbers and letters for quick communication.

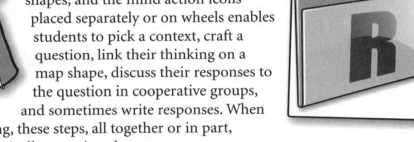

In early grades, teachers have charts showing examples of the questions from each of the seven thinking types. These charts are covered after the students have an understanding of the mind actions and can do them without the question starters. The examples can be viewed when necessary.

The displaying of ThinkTrix (matrix); the classroom curriculum contexts and ideas; the cognitive map; or ThinkLink, shapes, and the mind action icons placed separately or on wheels enables students to pick a context, craft a question, link their thinking on a map shape, discuss their responses to the question in cooperative groups, and sometimes write responses. When fully functioning, these steps, all together or in part, become a systemically engaging classroom.

▶ **Cubes and Die**—Students enjoy manipulating multisided objects to cue the mind actions. Larger cubes and smaller die meet this interest. Another cube or die can contain the departure points and even a third could contain contexts for study. Rolling all three of these cubes would be a transformed three-dimensional matrix. These cueing devices can be used with ThinkTrix board games. The outcome is deeper understanding of content—the ultimate purpose of all ThinkTrix activity.

▶ **Instructional Technology**—Teachers can use presentation software or an overhead projector to display text examples and to identify the thinking in the examples. This activity is particularly helpful in teaching the cognitive architecture of paragraphs. Some paragraphs are **Cause and Effect**, some are **Idea to Example**, and so forth. The text exemplars could also be test prompts or responses. Metacognitive unlocking, or unpacking, of questions and responses is a powerful skill for excelling on written assessments.

The teacher can use PowerPoint and software programs such as the cognitive mapping program "Inspiration" to clarify the thinking types. It is possible in some situations to use laptop response methods to cue or classify thinking. This instantaneous every-student-response (after Wait Time) allows students to learn from each other and for the teacher to check for their degree of understanding.

A ThinkTrix application could be designed to create icons next to student digitally written response to text. Note-taking then becomes a way for students to respond to text, not simply to repeat it. Each student response can be accompanied by the thinking types that constitute it.

Chapter 4

Cue Cards

Cue cards containing the seven mind actions can be used by the teacher or the students to identify how the mind is working or should work to answer or formulate a question, to solve a problem, make a decision, inquire, or create. They can be of any size depending on their use. When students can manipulate the cards, they have more ownership of the ThinkTrix metacognitive strategy.

RECALL

Cause and Effect

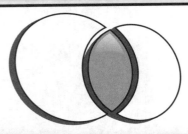

Similarity

Difference

Example to Idea

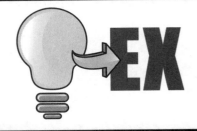

Idea to Example

Evaluation

ThinkTrix: Tools to Teach 7 Essential Thinking Skills
Kagan Publishing • (800) 933-2667 • www.KaganOnline.com

Wheels

Wheels with pointers are effective cueing devices, both handheld by students and displayable by the teacher. If each student has a wheel, every-student-response is facilitated in both total classroom and in cooperative groups. If the wheel has an outer rim displaying the focal points, approximating a matrix, the full effect of ThinkTrix is realized.

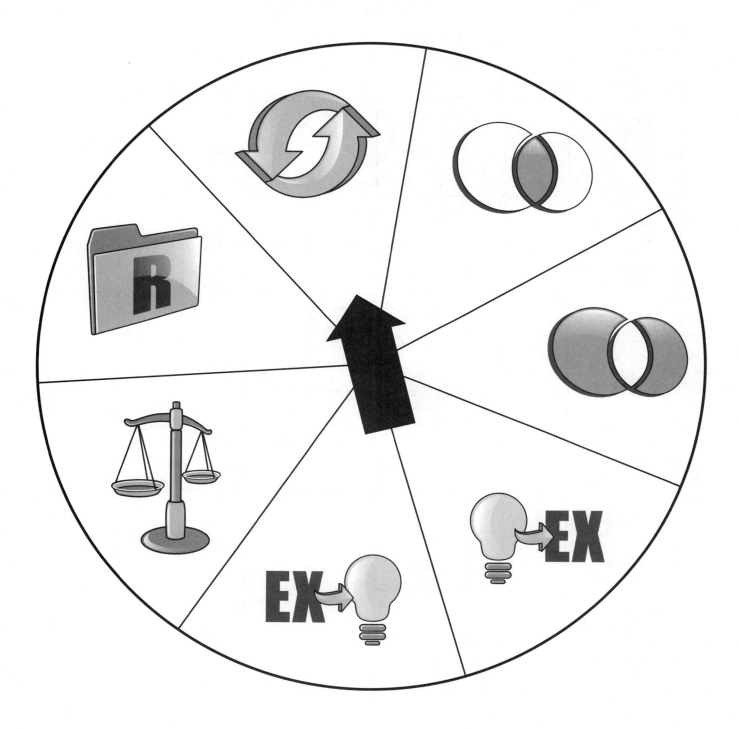

ThinkTrix Wall Chart

The fastest way for a teacher or student to refer to an intersection between a mind action and a focal, or departure point, is to have a large Wall Chart with each cell of ThinkTrix designated by number and letter. This focuses and engages an entire classroom as students or teacher craft questions on the spot. The two-sided ThinkTrix discussion boards are the most popular matrices with students, as they allow total student ownership of ThinkTrix facilitated discussion. Enlarge for wall use.

Focal Points

Subject	1)	2)	3)	4)	5)	6)	7)	8)
a) Recall	1a	2a	3a	4a	5a	6a	7a	8a
b) Cause and Effect	1b	2b	3b	4b	5b	6b	7b	8b
c) Similarity	1c	2c	3c	4c	5c	6c	7c	8c
d) Difference	1d	2d	3d	4d	5d	6d	7d	8d
e) Idea to Example	1e	2e	3e	4e	5e	6e	7e	8e
f) Example to Idea	1f	2f	3f	4f	5f	6f	7f	8f
g) Evaluation	1g	2g	3g	4g	5g	6g	7g	8g

Thinking Type

ThinkTrix: Tools to Teach 7 Essential Thinking Skills
Kagan Publishing • (800) 933-2667 • www.KaganOnline.com

Two-Sided Thinking Matrix

The two-sided ThinkTrix discussion boards are the most popular matrices with students, as they allow total student ownership of ThinkTrix facilitated discussion. Focal points can be filled in.

Source: Belinda Miller

THINK TRIX									THINK TRIX
Recall									Recall
Cause and Effect									Cause and Effect
Similarity									Similarity
Difference									Difference
Idea to Example									Idea to Example
Example to Idea									Example to Idea
Evaluation									Evaluation
THINK TRIX									THINK TRIX

Cueing = Inclusion

The signaling of thinking and other classroom interaction through mutually understood cueing systems is a major factor in including all students in the learning space. Everyone—school should be about everyone. For this goal to be reached, metacognitive understanding facilitated by interactive, or transactional, cueing systems is foundational.

Activities and Structures for ThinkTrix

Activities and Structures for ThinkTrix

We have seen how ThinkTrix expands the range of questions a teacher may ask of the class, and how cueing focuses students on the mind action(s) necessary to answer each question. Once the question is asked and the mind is focused on the appropriate mind action, the next step is to have students work alone or in small groups to grapple with the question—to construct their best answer.

In this chapter, we look at ways to structure the interaction among students to optimize their thinking. We examine the four ways students can work: individually, in pairs, in teams, or as a class. At each of these levels, there are many possible ways to structure interaction—many possible activities. This chapter offers sixteen powerful activities for students to ask and answer thinking questions.

Many of the structures herein are Kagan Structures. **Kagan Structures** are interactive instructional strategies. For more details on those structures and for dozens of additional structures that can be used in conjunction with ThinkTrix, see *Kagan Cooperative Learning* by Kagan Publishing. Just as ThinkTrix broadens the range of thinking; Kagan Structures broaden the range of ways to have students interact.

Individual activities encourage students to independently create their own questions and answer them. When finished, they can trade their questions with a partner. On a separate piece of paper, ThinkLink Map, or by using a One-Sided or Two-Sided ThinkTrix Discussion Board, students answer their partner's questions. After answering, partners can share what mind actions they used to answer each other's questions. Below are two Structures to use with ThinkTrix tools independently. See page 91 for steps on how to use the following activities.

Individual Activities

- Journal Writing
- Independent Answers

Pair activities allow students to work in pairs to generate questions to discuss with each other and sometimes to send to another pair. Partners take turns writing each question and also take turns recording each answer. After answering, pairs can join with other pairs to share how they answered the question, and partners share what mind actions they used to create and to answer each other's questions. Below are three Structures to use with ThinkTrix tools in pairs. See page 92 for steps on how to perform the following activities.

Pair Activities

- RallyRobin
- Pair Discussion
- Question-Record-Share-Discuss

Team activities allow students to work in teams to generate questions to send to another team. Teammates take turns writing each question and recording each answer. After answering, teams join to share how they answered the question. After answering, teams share what mind actions they used to answer each other's questions. Below are six Structures to use with ThinkTrix tools in teams. See pages 93–95 for steps on how to perform the following activities.

Team Activities

- Question Commander
- Fan-N-Pick
- Three-Step Interview
- Team Discussion
- Think-Pair-Square
- Question-Record-RoundRobin

Class activities provide opportunities for students to work (or play) with classmates. The classroom technique for students coming up with questions creates an inclusive classroom in which all students feel that they are important members. Students can trade their questions with a partner or in teams. Students can answer questions on a separate piece of paper, ThinkLink Map, with a ThinkTrix Discussion Board, or have a verbal discussion. After answering, partners or teams share with the class their answers and what mind actions they used to answer each other's questions. Below are five Structures to use with ThinkTrix tools in a classroom setting. See pages 96–98 for steps on how to implement the following activities.

Class Activities

- Mix-Pair-Discuss
- Think-Pair-Share
- Inside-Outside Circle
- Question & Answer
- Numbered Heads Together

Higher-Level-Thinking Questions Activities

Individual Activities

Activity #1

Journal Writing

Students individually create questions geared to journaling and place these on cards. The cards are distributed and students choose one Question Card. They then make a journal entry or use the question as the prompt for an essay or creative writing. Students then share their writing and what mind action(s) they used with a partner, or with teammates.

Activity #2

Independent Answers

Students each create their own set of Question Cards. Pairs or teams can share a set of questions, or the questions can be written on the board or Wall Chart. Students work by themselves to answer the questions in writing or with a ThinkLink Map, for each answer indicating which mind actions were used to create and answer the question. ThinkTrix tools such as the wheels or discussion boards are helpful for creating and **typing** the question. When finished, students can compare their answers with a partner, teammates, or the whole class.

Pair Activities

Activity #1

RallyRobin

Each pair gets a set of student-created Question Cards. ThinkTrix is used to create the questions. Student A in the pair reads the question aloud to his or her partner. Student B answers and shares the mind action he or she used. They can then compare the mind actions used to create and answer the question. Partners take turns asking, answering, and **typing/ classifying** each question.

Activity #2

Pair Discussion

Partners take turns asking questions created from the ThinkTrix icons or the discussion board. The pair then discusses the answers together and the mind action(s) used. Unlike RallyRobin, students discuss the answer. Both students contribute to answering and to discussing each other's thoughts.

Activity #3

Question-Record-Share-Discuss

One partner creates a question or uses a teacher-created question and reads the question aloud to his or her teammate. Both students write down their answers and the mind action(s) they used. Partners take turns sharing what they wrote. Partners discuss how their answers are similar and different.

Team Activities

Activity #1

Question Commander

Preferably in teams of four, students shuffle their ThinkTrix-created Question Cards and place them in a stack, questions facing down, so that all teammates can easily reach the Question Cards. Give each team a Question Commander set of instructions to lead them through each question.

Student #1 becomes the Question Commander for the first question. The Question Commander reads the question aloud to the team, then asks the teammates to think about the question, how they would answer it, and what mind action(s) they would use. After Think Time of at least 10 seconds, the Question Commander selects a teammate to answer the question and give the mind actions used. The Question Commander can spin a spinner wheel or roll a die to select who will answer. After the teammate gives the answer, Question Commander again calls for Think Time, this time asking the team to think about the answer. After Think Time, the Question Commander leads a team discussion in which any team member can contribute his or her thoughts, ideas, and mind actions used for the question, or give praise or reactions to the answer.

When the discussion is over, Student #2 becomes the Question Commander for the next question. This activity could center around question formation/creation as the task, with the cards containing topics or class contexts and the focus being on what mind action(s) would be necessary to answer the question created on the spot. Discussion of the answers to the question could follow. When the discussion is over, continue the activity with Student #3 and then Student #4 each becoming the Question Commander.

Activity #2

Fan-N-Pick

In a team of four, Student #1 fans out the Question Cards—student or teacher created, and says, *"Pick a card, any card!"* Student #2 picks a card and reads the question aloud to teammates. After 5 seconds of Think Time, Student #3 gives his or her answer including what mind action(s) was/were used. After another 5 seconds of Think Time, Student #4 paraphrases, praises, or adds to the answer and mind action(s) given. Students rotate roles for each new round. This activity requires a deep understanding of ThinkTrix mind actions.

Team Activities (continued)

Activity #3

Three-Step Interview

After a question is read to the team, students pair up. The first step is an interview in which one student interviews the other about the mind actions necessary to answer the question. In the second step, students remain with their partner but switch roles: The interviewer becomes the interviewee. In the third step, the pairs come back together to a foursome and each student in turn presents to the team what their partner shared concerning what mind action was used. Three-Step Interview is strong for individual accountability, active listening, and paraphrasing skills. Answers to the question and discussion of these answers may be incorporated in the activity.

Activity #4

Team Discussion

Team Discussion is an informal way of processing the questions and exploring ThinkTrix mind actions: Students read a question and then throw it open for discussion of the mind actions and the answers. Team Discussion, however, does not ensure that there is individual accountability or equal participation. A designated monitor helps in this regard, as does Think Time.

Activity #5

Think-Pair-Square

One student reads a question aloud to teammates. Partners on the same side of the table then pair up to discuss the question, their answers, and what mind actions are used. Then, all four students come together for an open discussion about the question. A two-sided game board may be used.

Activity #6

Question-Record-RoundRobin

Students take turns asking the team a question, using a ThinkTrix Two-Sided Game Board. After each question is asked, each student writes his or her thoughts on a piece of paper or on a ThinkLink Map. After students have finished writing, in turn, they share their answers. This format creates strong individual accountability because each student is expected to develop and share an answer and mind action for every question.

Chapter 5

Class Activities

Activity #1

Mix-Pair-Discuss

Each student gets a different Question Card, from a set created by the students from all the types of thinking on ThinkTrix. Some students may have the same question, which is OK. Students get out of their seats and mix around the classroom. They pair up with a partner. One partner reads his or her Question Card and the other answers, including what mind action(s) were used. Then they switch roles. When done, they trade cards and find a new partner. The process is repeated for a predetermined amount of time. The rule is students cannot pair up with the same partner twice. Students, however, may get the same questions twice or more, but each time it is with a new partner. This strategy is a fun, energizing way to ask and answer questions.

Activity #2

Think-Pair-Share

Think-Pair-Share is teacher directed. The teacher asks the question, and then gives students 3 to 10 seconds of Think Time, more if writing is cued. Students then pair up to share their thoughts about the question and the mind action(s) used to answer it. After the pair discussion, one student is called on to share with the class what was shared in his or her pair. This share mode should not be lengthy in that the purpose of the structure is maximum student engagement, not demonstration to the whole class. Shortening or even occasionally eliminating the whole class sharing brings the structure closer to Think-Pair-Square in student participation. There are times, however, when whole-class sharing is important. Also, students from kindergarten up can run Think-Pair-Share discussions.

Activity #3

Inside-Outside Circle

Each student gets a Question Card. Half of the students form an inside circle facing out. The other half forms a circle around the inside circle; each student in the outside circle faces one student in the inside circle. Students in the outside circle ask inside circle students a question. After the inside circle students answer the question and state what mind action(s) is used, students switch roles questioning and answering. After both have asked, analyzed, and answered a question, they each praise the other's answers and then hold up a hand indicating they are finished. When most students have a hand up, students trade cards with their partner and rotate to a new partner. To rotate, students in the outside circle move to the left. This format is a lively and enjoyable way to ask questions and have students listen to the thinking and mind actions of many classmates.

Activity #4

Question & Answer

This might sound familiar: Instead of giving students the Question Cards, the teacher asks the questions and after written or silent Think Time, calls on one student at a time to answer and state the mind action(s) involved. For example: *"That is a **Cause and Effect** question."* (This is not "cold call," rather "warm call," since Rehearsal Time is given before the student is called on.) This adjusted, traditional format eliminates simultaneous, cooperative interaction, but helps students develop their understanding of ThinkTrix mind actions. The teacher has the opportunity to spontaneously create the questions from the ThinkTrix icons, thereby modeling for the students what they do when they create their own questions.

Class Activities (continued)

Activity #5

Numbered Heads Together

Students number off in their teams so that every student has a number. The teacher asks a question. Students put their "heads together" to discuss the question including the mind actions. The teacher then calls a number and selects a student with that number to share what his or her team discussed.

Student-Generated ThinkTrix Questions

Student-Generated ThinkTrix Questions

Rationale

When students understand and recognize the seven types of thinking, teachers can encourage them to write their own questions, metacognitively, and to identify the types of thinking involved in answering questions asked in texts, on tests, and by others in the class. Once they learn to construct and classify questions using ThinkTrix, the students can write their own exercises and even tests. They can also discuss content in cooperative groups, while being fully aware of how they are thinking. In these situations they become active creators, not passive recipients of knowledge, and the self-motivated engagement in the classroom increases. Of course, the more intrinsically motivated the students are, through the relevance (to them) and the novelty of the content, the more likely it is that they will want to create and respond to questions. Students' natural curiosity, or the drive to know, is absolutely essential for metacognitive enfranchisement. The relevance of the content, or the sense that what they are learning is important to their lives, is equally essential. Curiosity and relevance engender response and persistence. Only when the drive to know and perceived relevance are in place along with the metacognitive skill to gain knowledge, can the students most effectively think critically and creatively about the curriculum. Learning is in direct relation to energized, mindful, and skillful student response to content.

Student-Generated Questions

Students who recognize, understand, and use the basic actions of the mind are ready for activities that accentuate the value of metacognition and increase achievement. The following structures are some that are effective in the gaining and deepening of this understanding and skill. Whereas metacognitive recognition of and practice with the seven thinking types is emphasized in the following activities, each activity may include the conversation that arises from the question or statement.

▶ **Matrix intersection**—In this activity, students individually or in pairs choose a cell on the matrix and create a question about the content. For instance, if the intersection is "Character" and **Example to Idea**, students could think of events in the character's experience and think of what character traits these events suggest.

▶ **Weird Facts RoundRobin**—In this activity, students see pictures of, or read about, novel events or phenomena and individually write questions using the seven mind actions. Each student shares the question and the others take turns identifying the type of mind action, justifying their classification, and discussing the fact. After everyone has had a turn, the questioner shares his or her classification.

▶ **Pair-Square-Agree**—In this activity, pairs of students decide on a question, ask it, and a facing pair comes to an agreement on what types of thinking are required to answer it. The square then seeks agreement on the question type. Discussion of the question follows.

▶ **Matrix Think-Match**—In this activity, students create questions using the matrix, give other students time to write down the grid cell that fits the question, and then the first students share the reason for their choice of the cell. The students match their thinking with that of the question maker(s) and discuss the choices. Discussion may follow any disagreement.

▶ **Free Type-Think-Match**—In this activity, students create questions about the content using only the seven thinking types and share the questions with the group. Students in the group then write down or pinch card the type of each question and match their thinking with that of the questioner. Discussion follows.

▶ **Type–Question–Think–Signal**—In this activity, a student creates a question from the seven thinking types, gives a hand signal for the other students to think of how they would classify the question, and then signals for a hand signal response from everyone. Each of the seven thinking types has a corresponding hand signal known to all the students. Discussion about matches and disagreements follows.

▶ **Pass a Question**—In this activity, a question is passed around a small group and each student writes down one icon or more to indicate the type(s) of thinking required to answer the question. In another variety, students write down the cell(s) on the matrix that the question fits. Different opinions can be discussed and questions answered.

▶ **ThinkTrix Board Consensus**—In this activity, two students sit facing each other with a two-sided ThinkTrix Matrix. They alternate making up questions from the cells and coming to agreement with their partners as to which matrix cell(s) fit the question. Discussion of the question follows.

▶ **Question Challenge**—In this activity, students in pairs or squares challenge each other to make up a given type of question. If the challenger doesn't agree with the **typing**, the question creator is asked to justify the classification. In a friendly competition, points may be awarded for classifications that meet the challenge. Students recognize that two different **typings** may be justifiable.

▶ **Test Design**—In this activity, using all seven ThinkTrix mind actions, students individually or in pairs design a test for each other or for another pair or the whole class. When taking the test, students are asked to write what type(s) of thinking they have to use to answer the question.

▶ **ThinkLink–ThinkTrix**—In this activity, students make up questions from ThinkTrix, and other students design cognitive maps, or ThinkLinks, that would best fit the answer. The ThinkLink shapes are chosen from a set of wall cues or are created.

▶ **RoundTable–Agree**—In this activity, one teammate spins a spinner containing the ThinkTrix icons and generates a question. If all teammates agree on its type, the question is recorded on the team question generator for use with the class or another team. Discussion of answers is expected.

▶ **AllRecord RoundRobin**—In this activity, each teammate takes turns rolling the die containing six of the ThinkTrix icons and generates a question. Then everyone records it. A variation is to have two dice, one with the icons and one with departure points for the question. As in all the activities, there is a list of contexts from which to choose a topic. The teacher often chooses the topic.

▶ **Jigsaw**—In this activity, there are home teams consisting of students who are each responsible for generating a question from one of the seven (or less) mind actions. With a created question, the students meet in specialty groups, each group focusing on one thinking type. In these groups, they share and discuss the question, coming to agreement that the questions are appropriately typed. Each student then returns to the home group prepared to defend at least two of the questions from the specialty group. A variation entails the student returning to the specialty groups with feedback from the home group.

▶ **Jot Thoughts**—In this activity, a team of students brainstorm questions using the matrix. They then decide which questions will produce the best thinking. When questions are chosen, teams take each other's questions, **type** them and discuss which questions will produce the best thinking.

▶ **Solo/Pair**—In this activity, students write questions independently using the Question Generator, the cubes, the die, wall cues, the spin wheel, the matrix, or the double-axis spin wheel. The teacher interacts with individuals. The next day, they share their questions and discuss the classifications with each other in pairs.

▶ **RallyTable with Consensus**—In this activity, pairs take turns writing the questions and checking for consensus.

Student practice writing out questions and discovering the thinking types in questions and text is essential for ThinkTrix fluency. This fluency enables students to know how their minds are working to solve problems, make decisions, inquire, and create. The samples of elementary students' work on the following pages illustrate the proficiency that they can achieve when they have working metacognition. All of the cognitive maps, or ThinkLinks, were created with certain thinking types in mind.

Student Examples

These fifth-grade students were learning how to translate test prompts into ThinkTrix types.

Worksheet 1:

In this column, copy the directions as they are stated on the MSPAP task.	Draw the symbol to represent the type of thinking used during the task	In this column, write to tell why or how you would use the think trix you chose.
Think about the water capac Think about the water holding capacit. Explain the suitability of the soil to sustain the structure	💡 → EX	The Idea is the suitabili The EX is if the house I stood up
Idea side creating a Perfect colony	💡 → EX	EX side How to creat a perect colony
Idea is to encourage them to move to the new Development	💡 → EX	EX How to encourage th
Idea is to make a brochure		
If you were going to add a Paragraph to the reading that describes problems related to too much or too little snowfall What information would you	💡	

Worksheet 2:

In this column, copy the directions as they are stated on the MSPAP task.	Draw the symbol to represent the type of thinking used during the task	In this column, write to tell why or how you would use the think trix you chose.
Explain the suitability of the soil to sustain the structure.	⚖️	We had to evaluate what the meaning of the structuas. And then evaluate if it sonded wright. And evaluat that it is suitbal.
	💡 — EX	💡 = To convince people to live in a new place. EX = Ideas to encourage people to Move.
	⨀ (venn)	The Diffrence is that, Your old home had more rooms and was bigger, but the new hoose wasn't. So they need to Modle the way the people want
If you were going to add a paragraph to the reading that describes problems related to too much or too little snowfall, what info. would you include?	💡 — EX	Because you have the idea that there is to much snowfall and then you list the Examples why.

Worksheet 3:

In this column, copy the directions as they are stated on the MSPAP task.	Draw the symbol to represent the type of thinking used during the task	In this column, write to tell why or how you would use the think trix you chose.
Explain the suitability of the soil to sustain the struture. *	↻	cause — suitabilty of soil effect — wether it stands.
Miss M said we didn't have to	EX →	The examples are the size people for the colony, naming it, and creating its culture. All these = a successfull colony
Miss M said we didn't have to	EX	EX — occupations, namely ect. the Great colony
If you were going to add a paragraph to the reading that describes problems related to too much or too little snowfall, what information would you include	☀ to EX	— benifits of snowfall EX — all the examples of Good snowfall

Student Example

This second-grader's story was an unassigned response from a ThinkTrix-proficient child who had been known to classify her parents' conversations with hand signals according to ThinkTrix mind actions.

"I love! Thanksgiving" said Jimmy.
"Me to" said Amy. "It is
wonderful" said Amy, "and it's a
BIG feast" added Jimmy.
"And you get sote fat" said
Jimmy. "You get yummy food."
Said Amy.
"Hey!" Said Amy. "we made a
cause and effect. The cause
is 'we eat a lot of food
on Thanksgiving. The effet is
we get sote fat. Then the
effect trns into the cause
now the cause is you get sote
fat on thanksgiving. and the effect
is we get skinyer again"

c   e→s,
Foody → fat e   skinny

Great story!

Student Examples

In the examples on the following pages, elementary students use the Question Generator to practice asking questions of all types.

FORMULATING MEANINGFUL QUESTIONS

Name: _____

Topic or Assignment: _____ Pocahontas _____

Question	Type	Questions
R	Recall	What was Pocahontas' son's name?
⬭	Same	How is John Smith similar to Cheif Powhaten?
⬭	Different	Explain how you think that the Native American God and the English's God are different.
↻	Cause/ Effect	What was the cause of Pocahontas to become fully Christian?
EX → 💡	Example to Idea	Thunder is an example of what thing to Cheif Powhaten.
💡 → EX	Idea to Example	Give some examples of how the Natives took care of the settlers.
⚖	Evaluate	Do you think it was good or bad of John Rolfe to take Pocahontas back to America.

Character   Story   Trait   Setting   Author's Style
Event   Feeling   Theme   Conflict   Relationship

Student Examples

Worksheet 1

FORMULATING MEANINGFUL QUESTIONS

Name: _____

Topic or Assignment: *Slave Dancer*

Question	Type	Questions
R	Recall	What instrument did Jessie use when playing music for the slaves?
(Venn - same)	Same	How was Jessie similar to Ras?
(Venn - different)	Different	How was Purvis different from the Captain?
(cycle arrows)	Cause/Effect	What was the cause of Jessie not liking music when he grew?
EX → 💡	Example to Idea	What idea was Jessie being kidn...
💡 → EX	Idea to Example	Give some exam... the sort of cloth... Jessie's mother
⚖	Evaluate	Do you think t... good or bad f... drown on the...

Character   Story   Trait   Setting

Event   Feeling   Theme   Confli...

Worksheet 2

FORMULATING MEANINGFUL QUESTIONS

Name: _____

Topic or Assignment: *Slave Dancer*

Question	Type	Questions
R	Recall	Where did Jessie live before he was kidnapped?
(Venn - same)	Same	Name at least two similarities between Purvis and Stout.
(Venn - different)	Different	What are some differences between Jessie's original home and the Moonlight?
(cycle arrows)	Cause/Effect	What drove the Americans to continue the slave trade?
EX → 💡	Example to Idea	The crew, the slaves, and harsh conditions were examples of what idea for Jessie?
💡 → EX	Idea to Example	Name 2 examples of the crew being unkind.
⚖	Evaluate	Was it right or wrong for Stout to beat Ras?

Character   Story   Trait   Setting   Author's Style

Event   Feeling   Theme   Conflict   Relationship

Student Examples

Name_____
Date_____

Example → Idea
Thinking

("Using examples to explain ideas!")

Helen Keller Movie → Thoughts

"When Helen touched the water, she suddenly realized what the ideas were. She already knew what the example was, but she needed clarification on what an idea for the meaning was. Helen found what W-A-T-E-R was when she connected the example to the idea and learned what the connection was." by Paul Lysko

"I think the example to idea thinking was at the end of the movie. Helen was given the example of what the things felt like and their signs. Then she got the idea that the signs were the names of the things."

These elementary students are examining the relationship between idea and example.

We often learn new ideas through seeing and experiencing examples of those ideas.

Name_____
Date_____

Explain another time when _____ learned through examples (yourself or another person).

Explain a time when Sean Fritz learned a new idea by seeing the examples of others.

(Homesick)

Trombone means the shiny thing in that box.

the alphabet

I saw my mom read the alphabet and so I finally got to reading it.
Ex. my self.

My next door neighbor is named Brett and boy pointing it a trombone and saying it. he copied and learned what it was.
Ex.

Ohio Michigan and others are states

The states would talk about states and tell about there families where she learnt the Tabz.
Ex.

Student Examples
1st Grade Story with Student Questions

Nancy Koza's first graders all recreated the *Three Billy Goats Gruff* story and created questions using ThinkTrix.

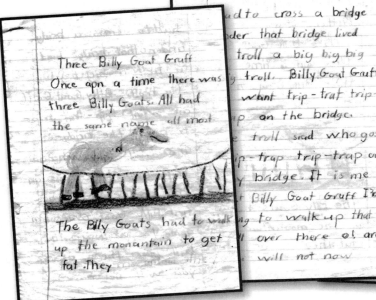

Three Billy Goat Gruff
Once apn a time there was
three Billy Goats. All had
the same name all most

The Billy Goats had to walk
up the monantain to get
fat. They

...ud to cross a bridge
...der that bridge lived
... troll a big big big
... troll. Billy Goat Gruff
... want trip-traf trip-
...p on the bridge.
...e troll said who gos
...ip-trap trip-trap on
...y bridge. It is me
... Billy Goat Gruff I'm
...ng to walk up that
...l over there o! are
...will not now

... going to eat you up
... the troll o! I'm so
... if you want my
... is coming he is
... biger then me
I will want
...our Brther so
... troll waned.
...lly Goat Gruff saw
... trip-trap trip-trap
...s trip-trap trip-
... is me Billy Goat
... for I'm going

...walk up that hill I
...there o! no your
...I'm going to eat
...p o! I'm so little
...want for my
...you can eat
...p he is much
...then me will
...can go then.
...ll waned then
...p trip-trap
...os trip-trap trip-
... is me great

Billy Goat Gruff
I'm going up that hill
over ther. o! no your
not I'm going to eat you
great Billy Goat Gruff
take his horns and
tossed the troll up in the
air and the troll
was became diad

(R) What did the tr...
to do?
the troll waeted t...
the Billy Goats.
(R) What are the na...
the Billy Goats?
there was Billy Goat...
Billy Goat Gruff to...
Great Billy Goat G...
(S) Why did the Bill...
walk up the mou...
the Billy Goats wa...
mountain to get fa...

(S) Why did the troll
laet a billy Goats go
because they were
little.
(T) What is the diffence
beten the trip-trap teps
One of the sists go vrey
slew and the other go
fast

Student-Led Questions/Responses
Belinda's Boys
Belinda Miller's 4th Grade Class

Below is a selection of questions asked between two fourth-grade boys, Ben and Joe. With a ThinkTrix Matrix between them, they chose, in a varied order, one or more contexts from a posted list of books, movies, and stories; a ThinkTrix mind action; and a departure point; and then they created a question. As each asked a question, he placed a marker on the intersecting cell of the matrix. When the other answered he placed a marker in the same cell. Each question was answered perceptively. The teacher, Belinda Miller, had just introduced ThinkTrix to the class in a single session. This video was the model for cooperative, student-centered, meaningful discussion and was the impetus for the spread of the ThinkTrix strategy to many clssrooms.

Ben and Joe sit on opposite sides of a ThinkTrix game board, referring to the stories and the matrix. Then they ask each other the following questions:

 "What was the similarity between the characters in The Great Brain *and* Run for the Blue Ribbon?*"* (**Similarity**/character)

 "What do you think was one of the good points about one of the characters in Run for the Blue Ribbon?*"* (**Evaluation**/character)

 "What do you think the theme of Run for the Blue Ribbon *was?"* (**Example to Idea**/story)

 "What was the key event in Things are Not Always as They Seem?*"* (**Example to Idea**, **Evaluation**/event)

 "What was one of the differences between Elliott in E.T. *and the boy in* Things are Not Always as They Seem?*"* (**Difference**/character)

 "What was the difference between Charlie's problem in Charlie and the Chocolate Factory *and the boy in* Run for the Blue Ribbon?*"* (**Difference**/problem)

 "What was the effect of the problem in Run for the Blue Ribbon?*"* (**Cause and Effect**/problem)

 "What was the cause of Indiana Jones going to the Temple of Doom?" (**Cause and Effect**/character)

Student–Led Questions/Responses
Thommie DePinto Piercy's 5th Grade Class

This is a verbatim account.

Cause and Effect
Student—What would happen if all the twelve men didn't come?
Teacher—(suggests clarification)
Student—All the twelve policemen.
Class correction—Sentries.
Student—All the twelve sentries.
Responses: • They, (he), would have gotten there faster
          • It would have gotten done faster.
          • They would have still had their horses.

Recall
Student—How many grandsons did Paul Revere have?
   Choral response—19

Idea to Example
Student—Give some examples of how Paul Revere was loyal?
Responses: • He took the messages to Philadelphia and he didn't stop.
          • He did the Midnight Ride.
          • He went to the Boston Tea Party.

Cause and Effect
Student—Why were the other messengers dispatched to longer routes?
Responses: • Because Paul Revere was going the same way as the
          British were going.
          • So what if Paul Revere didn't make it?

(continued)

Student-Led Questions/Responses
Thommie DePinto Piercy's 5th Grade Class *(continued)*

This is a verbatim account.

Idea to Example

Student—Give some examples of perseverance.

Responses: • He didn't quit.

• He finished his job when he got captured, and he just kept going when he had to walk.

• He didn't have a horse.

• Even though they caught him and let him go, he still did it.

• He went back and got the trunk.

Similarity/Difference

Student—How was he alike and different during and after the war?

Teacher—(suggests discussing "alike" first)

Responses: • He was busy.

• He was forgetful, he worked, and he helped people.

• He was still useful.

Cause and Effect

Student—What would happen to Paul Revere if he got caught on the Midnight Ride going across the Charles River?

Responses: • He would have been in trouble.

• He could have been executed or thrown in jail.

• He could have drowned.

• They might have taken him back to the king, and the people might have thought that he got through, and the people wouldn't be ready for the war, and we wouldn't have won.

Student-Led Questions/Responses
Thommie DePinto Piercy's 5th Grade Class

This is a verbatim account.

Example to Idea

Student—How do you think Paul Revere felt during the war?

Responses: • Nervous
- (Choral) Scared
- Because he didn't know if the Midnight Ride would work out or if he would be killed, or if he'd get caught.
- Nervous because when he rode, he could be scared that the British could get him.

Similarity

Student—How are Paul Bunyan and Paul Revere alike?

Responses: • (Choral) Same first name
- Both helpful
- Both men have perseverance.

Similarity

Student—How are the stories *Trumpet of the Swan* and *Paul Revere* alike?

Responses: • Both had perseverance
- I was thinking–ah–I forget–Chrystal knows. She answered it right, (during Think-Pair-Share).
- (Chrystal) The swan was busy playing his trumpet and he, (Paul), was busy with the war and stuff.

Cause and Effect

Student—What do you think would have happened if there was only one light shining in the church tower?

Responses: • Then they'd be coming by land.
- And he'd have to row quicker and the Midnight Ride would start quicker.

Student Questions

These questions were compiled by the teacher from student papers.

Upper Elementary   [≠]   Student Questions

Name two differences between Caleb Copeland and Ichabod Richardson. (char)
What is the difference between Boston and Joffrey? (setting)
What are some differences between the Richardson family and the Copeland family? (Char)
How is Amos different from Violet? (char)
What were the differences between Lydia and the white children? (char)
What are some differences between Amos'life in the Copeland's house and the Richard-
son's house? (char)
How are Mbui and sky man's actions different? (char)
What are some differences between you and Amos Fortune? (personal and char)
How were Etuk and Mbui different? (char)
How is Miguel different from his parents? (char)
What was the difference between "Mohawks" and "Mouse Woman's" Author style? (story)

Upper Elementary Student Questions [⟳]

What would have happened if Claudia ran away alone? (problem)
If Mr. Black hadn't existed how would the story be effected? (char. events)
Why did Claudia think that emptying the wastebaskets was a bad job? (char)
Would the story have changed if Claudia and James switched personalities? (char & Plot)
If Claudia and Jamie didn't find the file do you think Mrs. Frankweiler would have
told them? (char)
When the robot got lost what was the effect on Calvin?[⟳] Was the effect reasonable?
[EX → ?] (char)
Do you think Joffrey and/or its people changed during the time Amos lived there?(events)
When Amos freed Violet and married her how did it change Celyndia/s life? (event)
What caused Violet to bury the Iron Kettle with the money in it? (event)
What caused Amos to become a tanner? (char)
What was the effect of Amos not giving money to Louis? (char)
What was the effect of Amos being black? (char)
What was the effect of Polly's death of Ceylyndia? (problem-event)
Name some similarities and differences in why Kit and Amos came?
[⟳] then   [=] and [≠] (events)
What were the effects of Amos learning English, how to read, and reading the Bible? (char)
What were the similarities between why Amos and Kit had to come to America?
[⟳] then[=] (char and events)
Why does Amos free everyone? (event)
What was the effect of Mrs. Richardson's letter on Amos' feelings? (event)
What do you think caused Violet to bring back Amos' iron kettle? (char & event)
Although it isn't written, how do you think Amos' death effected the people of
Joffrey, mentally and physically? (problem-event)
Atlanta and Bola were both self-reliant. Why? (char)
If Mrs. Frankweiler had trusted Claudia and Jamie and just given them the paper by
Michael Angelo do you think they would have told the secret? Why or why not? (event)
What would have happened if Mbui didn't give the ball to the sky man? (event)
Why did the men shoot Sounder? (problem-event)
Fern talks to animals and they talk to her. Why do you think her parents did not
like this? (char-event)
Why does Wilbur feel it is gross for Charlotte to eat bugs? (clar- concept)
Why did Wilbur want to spin a web like Charlotte? (char, event)

Why did Fern's dad want to kill Wilbur? (char. problem)
What was the effect of Charlotte writing "Some Pig" in her web? (event - relationship)
Why does a nightingale's song sound better in the woods where he was raised than in the
Emperor's Palace? (relationship)
If Wilbur never met Charlotte, do you think he would have lived? (char-event)
Mr. Barby didn't seem to like Pony Rivers. Why? (char)

Student Questions

Upper Elementary 💡 → Ex.

What is an example of the idea hard work earns respect? (theme)
What traits did Amos have? (char)
Find some examples of how Amos never grows old. (char)
Give an example of fright in the story Foghorn. (concept)
What are some examples of Laurie being fresh to her father? (char, event)
Jonny had many problems. What were they? (problem)
What was an example of trust in Bando? (concept)
Old Ben was friendly. Give an example in the story to support this. (char)
What was an example of inference in the story "Bando?" (concept)
How did the second wife show love for Chief Saoks? (char)
Give me an example of loneliness in both stories.   Ex.   then   =   (concept)
What is the importance of your chosen theme? (theme)
If you could rewrite the Rules of Robotics, what would they be? (events)
How is this scenario unrealistic? (events)
Can you give an example of bravery on the part of Bogert? (theme-event)
What are some ways Amos got along well with whites? (char - events)
What is the good and bad part of Amos being taken from his tribe? (char - problem)
Explain some examples of related friendships in Amos Fortune and Witch of Blackbird Pond. (concept)
Give an example of a time when Kit acted like Amos Fortune. [=] then [💡→Ex.] (char-event
Find an example of personification. (concept)
Give some examples of how kind Amos is. (char-event)
What were the similarities of how both Amos and Kit had to get used to America?
[💡 → Ex.]   then   [=]   (char-events)

Upper Elementary   Ex. → 💡   Student Questions

Name one major theme of Little Lost Robot. (theme)
Who was more reasonable, Claudia or Jamie? (char)
Do you think that Violet was a nice person? If so, give some traits, if not give some traits. [Ex. → 💡]   then   [💡 → Ex.] (char)
What do you think is the most important theme in the story of Amos Fortune? (theme)
What is the main theme in Amos' life? (theme)
What do you think Kit would think of Amos? (char)
Amos has married two women who haven't lived long. Do you think he married them because he loved them or another reason? [Ex. → 💡]   and [🔃]   (char)
Claudia has found that she is rarely satisfied, and Jamie has found that he's been a tightwad. Do you think they want to change? [Ex. → 💡]   and [I²]   (char)
Mbui, Skyman, Etuk, Bush Cow, and crocodile are all examples. What is the idea? (char)
The idea is motives of the skyman, What are some examples? (char-events)

Was the Emperor's faking justified? (event)
Did Wilbur and Fern have a close relationship? (relationship-char)
When Jonny and Ponyboy rescued the children, Jonny died. How did Dolly feel about this? (event)
How is Theseus a hero? (char)
What kind of person was Mbui? (char)
What is the lesson to "By the Light of the Moon? " (theme)

Do you think it was smart of the stranger to leave the record there? (event)
Did the setting in "And Now Miguel" take place in a countryside? (setting)
Was Miguel brave to save the sheep? (char)
When the chief saw no meat and the finished blanket, what was his idea? (relationship)

Formulating
Meaningful Questions
All Grades Student Worksheet Sample—Math

Teacher demonstration Question Generator for Middle School Students

Topic or Assignment: _Graphing lines using M & B_   **Name:** _____

Question	Type	Questions
	Recall	Name the slope-intercept form for a line.
	Cause and Effect	Why are the slopes of these two equations "special?" $y - 6 = 0$ $2x + 8 = 0$
	Similarity	How are the following two equations the same? $2x + y = 6$ $y = 2x + 3$
	Difference	How are the slopes of these two equations different? $y - 6 = 0$ $2x + 8 = 0$
	Example to Idea	$y = 6$ is an example of a horizontal line. What is the "basic" equation for any horizontal line?
	Idea to Example	Parallel lines have the same slope and different y-intercepts. Can you give an example of two equations that meet these conditions?
	Evaluate	If you are given a linear equation to graph, why should you first write the equation in slope-intercepts form?

ThinkTrix: Tools to Teach 7 Essential Thinking Skills
Kagan Publishing • (800) 933-2667 • www.KaganOnline.com

Social Studies Sample Questions
Upper Elementary Student Questions

Using ThinkTrix, upper elementary students created these questions to share with the class as test items or in discussion. The icons next to the questions show the mind actions involved in answering the questions. Students made up the questions prompted with one selected mind action.

1. Do you think the story about Verrazzano being killed on the Island of Darien is what really happened? Why or why not?

2. Do you think that Henry Hudson had more successes or failures in his life?

3. Do you agree that Francisco Coronado went after an almost "hopeless dream"?

4. Which would you rather be: a Spartan woman or an Athenian woman?

5. If the Athenians had won the war, do you think their culture would be the same as it was before? Why?

6. Which civilization do you think is better, Athenian or Spartan? Why?

7. If the Athenians and the Spartans lived today, who would be more accepted by our culture? Why?

8. If you had an infinite supply of money, and you had to spend it on Sparta and Athens, what would you buy that was available in those times?

9. Which of these cultures were more advanced? Mycenae or Sparta and Athens or Crete.

10. Which civilization, Egypt, Greece, or Rome, was more technically advanced? Give examples.

11. If ancient Greeks didn't spend their money on homes, on what do you suppose they would spend their money?

12. If Aristotle taught Alexander the Great and Alexander conquered Greece, would you consider him a traitor? Why or why not?

13. Would you prefer being a Spartan boy or an Athenian boy? Explain why or why not.

14. Would you enjoy living in a Greek house? Explain why or why not.

15. What were some advantages of loving war?

16. Where would you have rather lived, Athens or Sparta? Why?

17. What one battle/war required the most military genius? Why?

18. Of Egypt, Mycenae, or Crete, where would you most like to live? Give five reasons.

19. What do you think Athens should have done to beat Sparta?

20. Who do you think was the most famous Athenian?

21. What steps would you take if you were the ruler of a civilization in chaos? How would you attempt to bring harmony?

22. Which is more similar to modern U.S.A., Athens or Sparta? Explain.

23. What were the advantages for the Native Americans in living near a river?

24. What were the disadvantages for the Native Americans in living near a river?

25. Do you think it was right or wrong for the settlers to come to colonize America?

26. Were palisades good protection or bad protection compared to our houses of today?

27. Was it good or bad for the settlers to come to Maryland?

28. Was it right for the settlers to take over the Indians' land?

29. Which of Archimedes' war machines do you think worked the best?

30. Was Hannibal's plan to defeat Rome by crossing the mountains a good one? Why?

31. If you were the Etruscan leader, would you have put a wall around Rome?

Social Studies Sample Quiz
Student-Generated Questions

 1. Who makes up the executive branch?

 2. If the president vetoes a law, how can it still get passed?

 3. Explain the difference between the main jobs of the judicial branch and the legislative branch of government.

 4. Making laws, collecting taxes, printing money, and maintaining the armed forces are all examples of what?

 5. List examples of the president's duties.

 6. In what building is the legislative branch located?

 7. Why do you think the president is the head of the armed forces, and only the Congress can declare war?

Source: Dawn Hanaway/Cooper Lane Traditional Academy

Elementary Student ThinkLink Examples

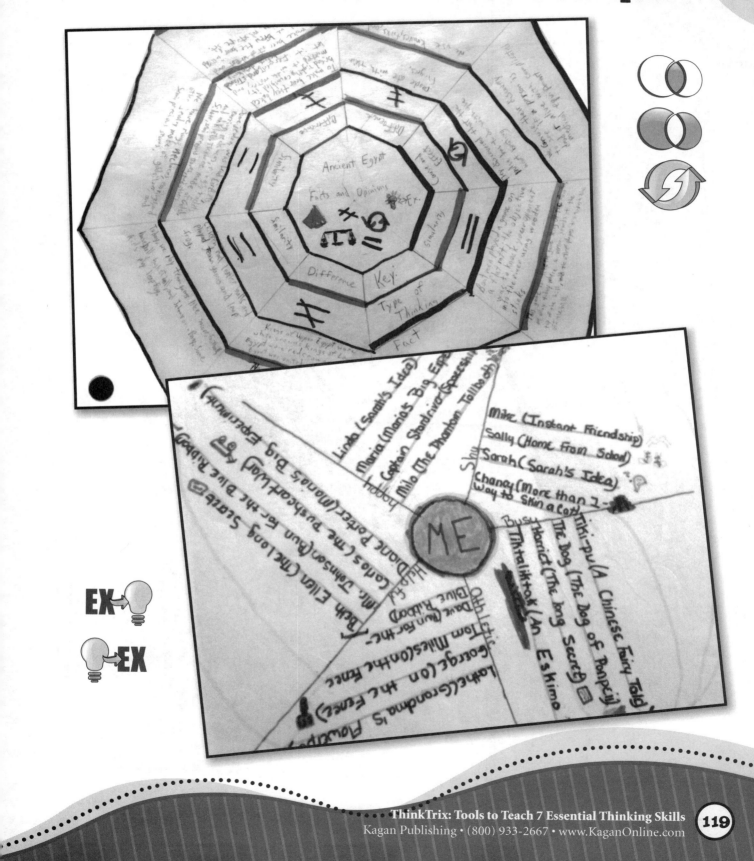

Elementary Student ThinkLink Examples

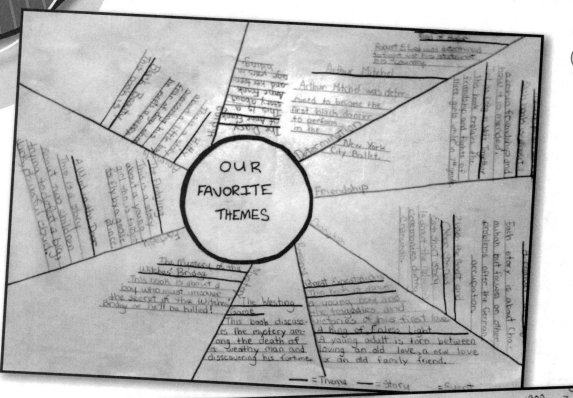

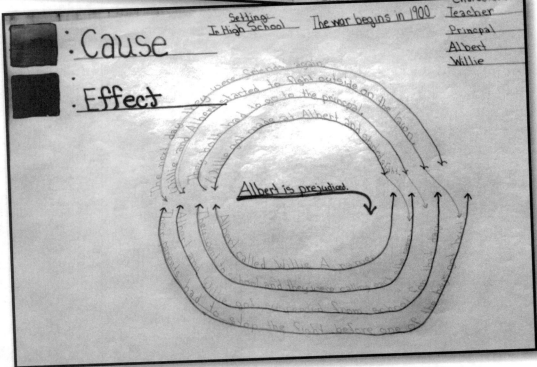

Elementary Student Wheel Example

From the question, *"How do students learn or what causes learning?,"* fifth-grade students constructed a theory and placed it on the wall.

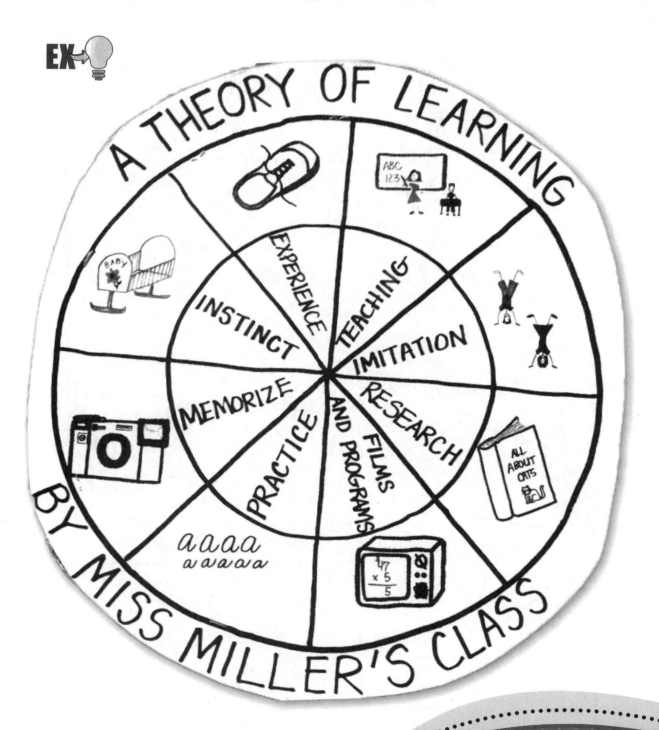

Elementary Student ThinkLink Example

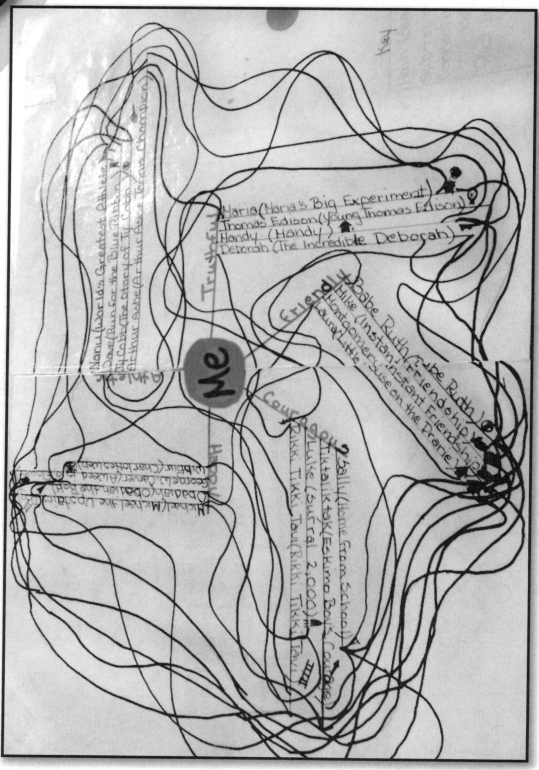

ThinkTrix: Tools to Teach 7 Essential Thinking Skills
Kagan Publishing • (800) 933-2667 • www.KaganOnline.com

Middle School Student ThinkLink Example

Students were encouraged to create ThinkLink designs.

A Cause-Effect Catapillar

A girl hits her cat.

The cat tries to get away from her and knocks over the bird cage

The door of the bird cage opens

The bird flies out the the window

The mother gives away the cat

The little girl is left without a pet

Elementary Student Poster Example
Shirley Rogers' 5th Grade Class

ThinkTrix: Tools to Teach 7 Essential Thinking Skills
Kagan Publishing • (800) 933-2667 • www.KaganOnline.com

Chapter 7

ThinkTrix Across the Curriculum

ThinkTrix Across the Curriculum

The Matrix

The term **ThinkTrix** was derived from a thinking matrix composed of two dimensions, one containing seven types of thinking and the other the departure points, or focal points, for the thinking. These departure points are the elements specific to the content area. For example, focal points in literature include character, setting, and conflict. Focal points in the visual arts include color, line, and space. The matrix was first intended as a question generator, then as a cooperative discussion tool for students. Teachers and students use the intersection of the thinking type and the content element to generate questions about any subject. The matrix, or ThinkTrix, can be a wall chart, a one- or two-sided desk tool, a pair of dice, a moving concentric parts wheel, a game board, or two sets of movable icons. The following descriptions are from four curriculum areas, though all other curriculum areas, such as art or music, could have a matrix as well. The teacher decides upon the content elements, or departure points. Whereas the descriptions are more consistent with classrooms grades 3–12, primary children can learn and use ThinkTrix at their level, using modified tools and hand signaling. Also, activities and tools in each description can be used in other curricular areas.

Language Arts, Literature, and Life

In the Language Arts classroom, metacognition is helpful to both reading and writing. The following description shows some ways that ThinkTrix tools can be used in Language Arts/Literature classes, elementary through secondary.

At all ages and levels, students can learn how to construct analogies from one context of literature or life to another. They can learn how to probe any event for causes and effects, sometimes analyzing cause and effect for significance in the story, sometimes generalizing beyond the story or life event. General questions such as *"What causes prejudice?" "What are the effects of jealousy?" "What leads to friendship?* are investigated by finding causes and effects in multiple contexts. Students and teachers generate and respond to questions of any type through natural curiosity or by using ThinkTrix tools such as the **Spinner Wheel**, the **WheelTrix**, **Movable Matrix Cards**, and the **Two-Sided ThinkTrix Boards**. Students prepare for cooperative learning by constructing questions independently first. The entire process is aided by visible lists of books, stories, film, and other contexts relevant to their lives. Using these student-derived lists as memory aides, students can "tease out" the universality of the events and themes.

ThinkLinks, or cognitive mapping, is an effective facilitator of deep thinking about literature and life. The "shaping" of the thinking makes the connections that reinforce and motivate the learning. Connections are made more indelible by the kinesthetic/visual experience of constructing cognitive maps. Characters are connected to characters, events to events, themes to themes, characters to their traits and feelings, and then ethical evaluations are made. The connections and the questions that make insight possible are facilitated by the students' and teacher's conscious awareness and labeling of the types of thinking being employed. Students can use the completed cognitive maps as discussion guides or as "blueprints" for written composition. Various cognitive map shapes are placed in view and the teacher encourages students to create their own designs. From the activities, students create wall lists of traits, feelings, ideas, and themes. The teacher and students use these lists to enrich discussion. Aided by their knowledge of ThinkTrix mind actions, students learn how to question and how to construct responses. The relevance of Language Arts/Literature to their lives becomes apparent through an understanding of the workings of the mind and the conversations arising from this awareness.

ThinkTrix Matrix
Literature

The framework of thinking may be visualized as a matrix with one axis representing the focal points, and the other axis representing the thinking types, or mind actions, involved. This framework is useful for reminding teachers and students of questions to ask and types of responses to make. The focal points below are examples of what might be appropriate for reading/literature. They may be changed depending on content area or learning objective.

Focal Points

Thinking Types	1) Character	2) Event	3) Feeling/ Trait/ Theme	4) Story	5) Setting	6) Problem/ Conflict	7) Author's Style	8) Relationship
a) Recall								
b) Cause and Effect								
c) Similarity								
d) Difference								
e) Idea to Example								
f) Example to Idea								
g) Evaluation								

Two-Sided ThinkTrix Discussion Board
Literature

Directions: Students, individual(s) or in pairs, sit on opposite sides of the board. Students on one side ask a question and place a marker on the cell(s) that prompted it. Students on the other side confirm or doubt the classification and try to answer. Discussion follows. Alternating back and forth, students on the other side frame a question and begin the process again. The focal points are written and placed on both sides of the board.

Literature / THINK TRIX	Relationship	Author's Style	Problem/ Conflict	Setting	Story	Feeling/Trait/ Theme	Event	Character	THINK TRIX / Literature
Recall									**Recall**
Cause and Effect									**Cause and Effect**
Similarity									**Similarity**
Difference									**Difference**
Idea to Example									**Idea to Example**
Example to Idea									**Example to Idea**
Evaluation									**Evaluation**
Literature / THINK TRIX	Relationship	Author's Style	Problem/ Conflict	Setting	Story	Feeling/Trait/ Theme	Event	Character	**THINK TRIX / Literature**

Two Sided ThinkTrix Discussion Board
Language Arts

Directions: Students, individual(s) or in pairs, sit on opposite sides of the board. Students on one side ask a question and place a marker on the cell(s) that prompted it. Students on the other side confirm or doubt the classification and try to answer. Discussion follows. Alternating back and forth, students on the other side frame a question and begin the process again.

Language Arts THINK TRIX	Reading	Writing (Composition)	Vocabulary	Grammar	Spelling	Word Origin	Imagery	Story Telling	THINK TRIX Language Arts
Recall									Recall
Cause and Effect									Cause and Effect
Similarity									Similarity
Difference									Difference
Idea to Example									Idea to Example
Example to Idea									Example to Idea
Evaluation									Evaluation
Language Arts THINK TRIX	Reading	Writing (Composition)	Vocabulary	Grammar	Spelling	Word Origin	Imagery	Story Telling	THINK TRIX Language Arts

ThinkTrix: Tools to Teach 7 Essential Thinking Skills
Kagan Publishing • (800) 933-2667 • www.KaganOnline.com

Meaningful Mathematics

In the Mathematics classroom, beyond skill with calculations, students are encouraged to know the meaning, or the concepts, behind the processes. Meaning can take the form of a concrete understanding of the operations and the problem solving, as well as relevance—a practical understanding of the uses of the math. The ThinkTrix strategy adds a third and meta dimension to meaningful mathematics. With a working knowledge of the seven mind actions, or thinking types, the students are aware of how the mind has to work in order to do and understand mathematics.

Though skill at operations, recall of facts and formulae, and problem-solving methods are essential to success in mathematics, students benefit by knowing how their minds work as they apply methods and skills. This mathematical metacognition can be achieved by using a blank math matrix as a tool. Once they understand the thinking types of ThinkTrix, students at all levels are capable of filling in a blank matrix with questions in each cell. This capability is highly motivating because they can create their own assignments and tests. To bring students to this capability, the teacher models a filled-in mathematics ThinkTrix grid. Once they have discussed the model in cooperative groups, individuals fill in the cells of a blank grid with their own questions and then quiz each other in groups. As each question is examined, students name the thinking type or types being used to answer it.

After practicing "question making" using the teacher's model several times, students try the exercise with a blank matrix only. They work independently and then check their questions with a partner. During these practice exercises, the teacher interacts with students, asking them for their reasoning in placing a question in a given cell. When students have shown proficiency at filling in the grid, the teacher has each student create a test to share with a partner or a team of four. Students are now test makers, not merely test takers.

When students are proficient at creating and labeling the questions and answers, the teacher can ask them to label with wheels or pinch cards any question or problem-solving step. Also, the teacher can reinforce the metacognitive concepts by orally translating all questions as to the mind action required to respond. This is done by using the language of ThinkTrix as part of all prompts and questions. Through these activities and the clarity achieved through a common understandable set of terms, a third level of meaning in mathematics is achieved—a level of shared metacognition.

ThinkTrix Matrix
Mathematics

The framework of thinking may be visualized as a matrix with one axis representing the focal points, and the other axis representing the thinking types, or mind actions, involved. This framework is useful for reminding teachers and students of questions to ask and types of responses to make. The focal points below are examples of what might be appropriate for mathematics. They may be changed depending on content area or learning objective.

Focal Points

	1) Number	2) Set	3) Operation	4) Algorithm	5) Relationship	6) Property	7) Concept/ Rule/ Axlom/ Theorem	8) Problem
a) Recall								
b) Cause and Effect								
c) Similarity								
d) Difference								
e) Idea to Example								
f) Example to Idea								
g) Evaluation								

Thinking Types

Two-Sided ThinkTrix Discussion Board
Mathematics

Directions: Students, individual(s) or in pairs, sit on opposite sides of the board. Students on one side ask a question and place a marker on the cell(s) that prompted it. Students on the other side confirm or doubt the classification and try to answer. Discussion follows. Alternating back and forth, students on the other side frame a question and begin the process again. The focal points are written and placed on both sides of the board.

Mathematics THINK TRIX	Problem	Concept/ Rule/Axiom/ Theorem	Property	Relationship	Algorithm	Operation	Set	Number	THINK TRIX Mathematics
Recall									Recall
Cause and Effect									Cause and Effect
Similarities									Similarities
Differences									Differences
Idea to Example									Idea to Example
Example to Idea									Example to Idea
Evaluation									Evaluation
Mathematics THINK TRIX	Problem	Concept/ Rule/Axiom/ Theorem	Property	Relationship	Algorithm	Operation	Set	Number	THINK TRIX Mathematics

ThinkTrix
Probability Teacher Questions
Sample Worksheet
by Suzanne Levin-Weinberg

Question Type	Example
Recall	Add 3 + 4; define fraction.
Cause and Effect	Show how to make three equal groups with 15 counters. What would you do if you started with 16 counters?
Similarity	How are improper fractions and mixed numbers alike?
Difference	When would we use an improper fraction as opposed to a mixed number?
Idea to Example	We use a ratio to compare two quantities. Give an instance where you have seen a ratio.
Example to Idea	44, 36, 100, 81, 625 are all examples of…?
Evaluation	Is it easy to mentally compute or estimate 27 • 23? Why?

Directions: Read the following problems. Classify each one with ThinkTrix thinking types. Then, answer each question. Work in pairs. (Answers provided in the form of symbols.)

Question	Type

1. Begin simple. Consider the die. It has six different numbers on it!
  A. What is the probability of the die landing with an even number on top P(x = even)?
  B. What is the probability of the die landing with a number greater than 3 on top P(x > 3)?
  C. What is the probability of the die landing with a number greater than or equal to 3 on top P(x ≥ 3)?	

2. Now suppose the die is changed. Instead of having all of the numbers from 1–6 on the die, the die now has the numbers 2–6, and the number 4 is on the die twice! Repeat the questions in problem 1.	
3. The number facing up on a die is a random event. That is, if we throw a 2, then the probability of throwing another 2 is still 1/6. List another example of a random event.	
4. Let's look now at our pattern blocks. We have five shapes: a green triangle, an orange square, a blue rhombus, a red trapezoid, and a yellow hexagon. What is the probability of picking the blue rhombus P(x ≠ blue rhombus)? What do you notice about these two events?	
5. Write a general rule which summarizes what happened in problem 4.	
6. Consider the two events: P(x = green shape) and P(x = blue shape). How are these two events the same as the two events in problem 4? How are these two events different from the two events in the problem?	
7. We call the two events in problem 4 "complementary" events. Complementary events exist all over the place. Give two examples of other complementary events.	

8. What do you think the probability of these events are? Write a sentence explaining your answer to each one.
  A. P (Professor Levin loves snowball fights) = _____
  B. P (Picking a 5-sided shape from the pattern blocks) = _____
  C. P (Picking a primary color from the pattern blocks) = _____	

ThinkTrix: Tools to Teach 7 Essential Thinking Skills
Kagan Publishing • (800) 933-2667 • www.KaganOnline.com

ThinkTrix
Primary Math Teacher Sample

Directions: Teacher and students may build a ThinkTrix model together.

Source: Nancy Koza

	Numbers and Numeration	Collecting and Organizing Data	Whole Number Operations	Geometry	Fractions	Measurement	Money
	What number comes after 25?	What is a bar graph?	What is the sum of 3 plus 4?	How many sides and corners does a triangle have? Draw a circle.	How many pieces would I have if I cut this apple in half?	How long is this paper? How many inches are in a foot?	Name the coins.
	What would happen if I removed one member from this set?	Why are graphs important?	If 1 + 9 = 10, what would 10 + 90 equal?	What shapes could you use if you wanted to draw a house?	What would happen if you were measured for new shoes using a nonstandard unit of measure?	If it is 4:00, what time will it be in 2 hours?	What could you buy if you had $1.00?
	Which sets have the same number of members? How are these sets the same? XXX OOO ▲▲▲	What is the same about circle graphs, bar graphs, and line graphs?	Compare these number sentences. 1 + 3 = 4 • 4 - 1 = 3 3 + 1 = 4 • 4 - 3 = 1	How are a square and a rectangle the same?	How are these fractional parts the same?	Find two non-standard units of measure that are the same length.	Which coins are silver?
	How are these sets different? XX XXX	How do circle graphs, line graphs, and bar graphs differ?	How is the process of addition different from the process of subtraction?	How are a square and a rectangle different?	How is 1/3 different from 1/4?	Find the tallest tree in the schoolyard.	How are a nickel and a dime different?
	Name some odd numbers.	What kinds of problems might you have in collecting data for our project?	How many ways can you show a set of 6? What are some facts that equal 10?	Give some examples of 4-sided figures. Show some examples of closed curves.	Show some examples of halves.	Show some examples of calendars. What kinds of tools do we use to measure length?	What kinds of problems might you have if you didn't have any money?
	Are 2, 6, and 12 examples of even numbers?	Bar graphs, line graphs, and circle graphs are all ways of _____	6 – 3 is an example of what kind of whole number operation?	You have added three more shapes to the pattern. Are they correct?	These pictures are examples of what fractional part?	A tape measure, yardstick, and inch stick can all be used to measure _____.	Name some reasons for knowing about making change.
	Did _____ place these numbers in order?	What graph would you use to organize your data? Why?	What operation will you need to use to solve this problem?		Did _____ cut this shape into equivalent pieces?	Was _____ to use a ruler as the fastest way to measure your room?	Do you have enough money to buy a watch?

ThinkTrix
Middle School Math Teacher Sample

Directions: This Math ThinkTrix was designed by Barbara Hoffman, a middle school math teacher, and is an example of a teacher adapting ThinkTrix to a special situation. Focal points may always be changed to suit the situation. This matrix can be enlarged for large group discussion.

Source: Barbara Hoffman

	a) Recall	b) Cause and Effect	c) Similarity	d) Difference	e) Idea to Example	f) Example to Idea	g) Evaluation
1) Whole Numbers	1a	1b	1c	1d	1e	1f	1g
2) Fractions/Decimals	2a	2b	2c	2d	2e	2f	2g
3) Statistics/Graphing	3a	3b	3c	3d	3e	3f	3g
4) Ratio/Proportion/Percent	4a	4b	4c	4d	4e	4f	4g
5) Integers	5a	5b	5c	5d	5e	5f	5g
6) Geometry	6a	6b	6c	6d	6e	6f	6g
7) Measurement	7a	7b	7c	7d	7e	7f	7g
8) Computers	8a	8b	8c	8d	8e	8f	8g

ThinkTrix: Tools to Teach 7 Essential Thinking Skills
Kagan Publishing • (800) 933-2667 • www.KaganOnline.com

ThinkTrix
Sample Math Questions
by Barbara Hoffman

Question cues have been used effectively by many teachers. Begin by using the symbols to derive your questions as you are discussing a topic with a group or class. Gradually let the students in on the "secret" of your questioning. "R" type questions are usually best to start with since students can easily remember that "R" stands for **Recall**. The next step would be to teach the students how to use some of the symbols to make up questions. This encourages metacognition (thinking about your own thinking). Follow-up by encouraging students to categorize questions and responses according to type. When you are satisfied with their facility in using the cues, you can create a grid of ThinkTrix in your content area, which you and your students may use as an oral, diagrammatic, and written question-or-response generator.

As with any other teaching strategy, it will be effective only if it is utilized regularly. Asking questions of different types can be facilitated by mounting cards with the cue symbols on the classroom walls as visual reminders to everyone.

Sample Questions for Math ThinkTrix

Thinking Type	Questions
Recall	How many degrees are there in a straight angle? Name the different parts of a fraction.
Cause and Effect	What would the result be if you multiplied a number by its reciprocal? What effect will computers have on our society? Our school?
Similarity	Compare .27 to 27%. How are a parallelogram and a trapezoid alike?
Difference	List three functions that a human can perform that a computer cannot and three functions that a computer can perform that a human cannot. Contrast an equilateral pentagon with a square.
Idea to Example	What are some examples of a mixed number? Draw three examples of a quadrilateral.
Example to Idea	What are the following all examples of: 3n, 2n + 4, a + 2b, n/4, 3x − 2? In the following examples, what does the underlined number represent? 3.0$\underline{2}$4, 4$\underline{2}$.6592, 36$\underline{2}$.10
Evaluation	Do you think bar graphs or frequency tables show information more accurately? Rate your classroom performance in this class.

Science through Inquiry

Science relies on the drive to know. An ally of curiosity is metacognition—knowing how we think. The Science classroom at all levels is about acquiring knowledge and learning how to create knowledge through inquiry. In a science learning environment, students analyze data, make and attempt to prove or disprove hypotheses, and accumulate knowledge. To be more effective in acting as scientists, students use ThinkTrix to become consciously aware of how their minds work as they think. Are the data to be organized by **Similarity** or **Difference**? Does the hypothesis deal with cause or effect or both **Cause and Effect**? Should the hypothesis precede the data (**Idea to Example**) or derive from the data (**Example to Idea**)? How should the hypothesis be confirmed (**Idea to Example**)? **Evaluation** comes into play to assess the ethical dimensions of certain scientifically generated propositions or theory and the means used to come to these conclusions. When the research is completed, how should it be organized for **Recall**?

In cooperative groups, students identify and track the actions of their minds as they engage in scientific thinking. They use ThinkTrix tools to do the thinking and to reflect upon it afterwards. They are able to formulate the questions and to identify how they should think to search for answers. Following all individual inquiry and the experimenting, observing, listening, or reading, students reflect collaboratively upon what they are learning. From case studies such as Newton and the Apple (**Example to Idea**), to their own attempts to unlock the concepts and principles embedded in discrepant phenomena, they reflect back to each other how the mind worked to examine the data and arrive at insights.

Students accomplish this cooperative reflection by using ThinkTrix tools. They can fill in the cells of a **Science ThinkTrix Grid**; use the **Handheld Thinking Wheel** or **Pinch Strips** to identify the mind actions; use the **Two-Sided Science ThinkTrix** to come to consensus on content and thinking types; identify or follow the thinking steps on the **Problem-Solving Flowchart** as an experiment is being designed; using "Science Buddies" or "Discovery" on the Internet, identify the types of thinking involved in science projects; design ThinkTrix-coded cognitive maps to generate, organize, and recall knowledge; use the Science ThinkTrix Grid to construct test questions.

Science requires certain paths of thought, a clear concept of what these paths are, and of what actions of the mind they consist. Facility with ThinkTrix and its tools will make these paths, or processes, of thought and their stages, indelible and useful for students. Thinking from data to hypothesis and from hypothesis to data and knowing you are doing it is crucial to successful scientific inquiry. Aided by the knowledge of ThinkTrix, students can more easily do what scientists do, know how they are doing it, and remember how to act scientifically in the future.

ThinkTrix Matrix
Science

The framework of thinking may be visualized as a matrix with one axis representing the focal points, and the other axis representing the thinking types, or mind actions, involved. This framework is useful for reminding teachers and students of questions to ask and types of responses to make. The focal points below are examples of what is appropriate for science and may be changed depending on content area or learning objective.

Focal Points

Thinking Types	1) Person	2) Object	3) Environment	4) Event	5) Phenomenon	6) System	7) Concept/ Hypothesis/ Theory	8) Relationship
a) Recall								
b) Cause and Effect								
c) Similarity								
d) Difference								
e) Idea to Example								
f) Example to Idea								
g) Evaluation								

Two-Sided ThinkTrix Discussion Board
Science

Directions: Students, individual(s) or in pairs, sit on opposite sides of the board. Students on one side ask a question and place a marker on the cell(s) that prompted it. Students on the other side confirm or doubt the classification and try to answer. Discussion follows. Alternating back and forth, students on the other side frame a question and begin the process again.

THINK TRIX Science	Person	Object	Environment	Event	Phenomenon	System	Concept/ Hypothesis/ Theory	Relationship	THINK TRIX Science
Recall									Recall
Cause and Effect									Cause and Effect
Similarity									Similarity
Difference									Difference
Idea to Example									Idea to Example
Example to Idea									Example to Idea
Evaluation									Evaluation
THINK TRIX Science	Person	Object	Environment	Event	Phenomenon	System	Concept/ Hypothesis/ Theory	Relationship	THINK TRIX Science

ThinkTrix: Tools to Teach 7 Essential Thinking Skills
Kagan Publishing • (800) 933-2667 • www.KaganOnline.com

ThinkTrix
Science Teacher Sample

Directions: Teachers can design grids to fit their individual programs. For example, in this sample grid, the teacher added **Big Idea to Little Idea** and created a mind action icon (I → i) to help students recognize and recall the mind action.

	Problem	Hypothesis	Materials	Procedure	Observation	Conclusion	Theory	Fact	Discipline Pure vs. Applied	Negative Effects	Positive Effects	Event	Process or Sequence	Unknown or Unexplained	Insight and Intuition
I → i Big Idea to Little Idea															
Evaluation															
EX Example to Idea															
EX Idea to Example															
Difference															
Similarity															
Cause and Effect															
Recall															

Life Science
Biocommunities Teacher Sample

Directions: Teacher and students may build a ThinkTrix model grid together.

	Recall	Cause and Effect	Similarity	Difference	Idea to Example	Example to Idea	Evaluation
Organisms	Name some microscopic organisms in the pond.	What might be the effect of introducing a new species into an established pond?	Compare the life cycle of a mosquito to that of a dragon fly.	Describe how a tadpole is different from a frog.	List some reasons for the importance of beavers.	What are some traits of an amoeba?	Do you agree that all organisms are important for a balanced ecosystem?
Populations	Tell what a population is of a pond.	Predict what would happen if the population of a pond became unbalanced?	Explain how populations of a pond and a swamp are alike.	Contrast the populations of living organisms in a clean pond to those living in a pond affected by acid rain.	What are some examples of problems of over-population.	What conclusions can you draw about the importance of a well-balanced pond?	In your opinion, should natural ponds be stocked with an abundance of fish?
Food Chains	Which organism is at the beginning of any food chain in a pond?	Diagram the effects of each step of the food chain.	Compare two different food chains in a pond.	Contrast two different food chains in a pond.	Give some examples of energy being transferred through a pond's food chain.	Based on the examples, what are some requirements of all food chains?	Is one segment of the food chain more important than the others? Explain.
Environments	State two ways people use ponds.	How does air pollution affect a pond?	Describe how pond and swamp ecosystems are alike.	The pond environment is different from a swamp environment. Explain.	The pond's environment is made up of what elements?	The pond environment has unique qualities. Name two.	What do you think should be done about acid rain?
Consumers	What are consumers?	What is the effect of having consumers in a pond?	How are consumers in a pond and a swamp similar?	Contrast the importance of a consumer with that of a decomposer.	What are some examples of consumers?	What is the most important characteristic of all consumers?	Do you agree that consumers are important for a balanced ecosystem?

ThinkTrix: Tools to Teach 7 Essential Thinking Skills
Kagan Publishing • (800) 933-2667 • www.KaganOnline.com

Social Studies and Society

The Social Studies classroom is a laboratory for understanding the behavior and history of people in and among their societies and cultures. To develop this understanding, students need to think critically and creatively. The following description shows how ThinkTrix and the associated tools can aid the thinking necessary to gain knowledge and to persist in learning more.

As is true in science, learning in social studies often is best facilitated by discrepant events or cognitive incongruities. Curiosity is the prerequisite for student motivation and for persistence in learning. At the same time, indelible events become nodes of the structure of knowledge that connects facts, concepts, and generalizations. Case studies that have astounding content are the "islands" to return to as students try to understand the myriad events that shape human interaction and history. As students think about societal phenomena and history, their ability to comprehend and use the knowledge is enhanced by an understanding of how their minds work as they think.

After students learn the seven mind actions of ThinkTrix and how to use the several ThinkTrix tools that facilitate question and response, they are ready to approach the course content in a more mindful way. They then can inquire into **Cause and Effect**, discern and make analogies, conceptualize or generalize from **Example to Idea**, support **Idea to Example**, make distinctions by finding differences, and evaluate according to positive and negative effects, or consequences—all in a conscious way. **Two-Sided ThinkTrix Discussion Boards** can be used to encourage cooperative dialogue; the **Spinner Wheel** can be used with two or more students to encourage spontaneous thinking about discrepant events or phenomena; **Double ThinkTrix Wheel** can be used with cognitive map shapes to organize the thinking the students do, and with the **WheelTrix**, students can design questions for classroom tests or for asking other students in cooperative groups. All activities may include writing.

In short, students can learn to "reconnoiter" over the data as an historian or anthropologist would do. They become mindful of the process of historical and social inquiry, and of its importance in building their structures of knowledge.

ThinkTrix Matrix
Social Studies

The framework of thinking may be visualized as a matrix with one axis representing the focal points, and the other axis representing the thinking types, or mind actions, involved. This framework is useful for reminding teachers and students of questions to ask and types of responses to make. The focal points below are examples of what is appropriate for social studies and may be changed depending on content area or learning objective.

Focal Points

Thinking Types	1) Person	2) Event/Fact	3) Place	4) Story/ Extended Event	5) Concept/ Generaliza- tion/Theory	6) Culture	7) Problem/ Conflict	8) Relationship
a) Recall								
b) Cause and Effect								
c) Similarity								
d) Difference								
e) Idea to Example								
f) Example to Idea								
g) Evaluation								

ThinkTrix: Tools to Teach 7 Essential Thinking Skills
Kagan Publishing • (800) 933-2667 • www.KaganOnline.com

Two-Sided ThinkTrix Discussion Board
Social Studies

Directions: Students, individual(s) or in pairs, sit on opposite sides of the board. Students on one side ask a question and place a marker on the cell(s) that prompted it. Students on the other side confirm or doubt the classification and try to answer. Discussion follows. Alternating back and forth, students on the other side frame a question and begin the process again.

Source: Renee Brinfield

THINK TRIX Social Studies	Relationship	Problem/ Conflict	Culture	Concept/ Generalization/ Theory	Story/ Extended Event	Place	Event/Fact	Person	THINK TRIX Social Studies
Recall									Recall
Cause and Effect									Cause and Effect
Similarity									Similarity
Difference									Difference
Idea to Example									Idea to Example
Example to Idea									Example to Idea
Evaluation									Evaluation
THINK TRIX Social Studies	Relationship	Problem/ Conflict	Culture	Concept/ Generalization/ Theory	Story/ Extended Event	Place	Event/Fact	Person	THINK TRIX Social Studies

ThinkTrix
High School Social Studies
Teacher/Student Sample

Directions: Students and teacher may build a ThinkTrix model together.

Source: Renee Brimfield

	Social	Political	Economic	Diplomatic	Military
Recall				Which country was a major ally of the United States during the latter part of the Revolution?	
Cause and Effect	Why did many slaves fight for the British?				
Similarity		When the First and Second Continental Congresses first met, they both did what?			
Difference					Which country's military was considered weaker at the start of the war? In what ways?
Idea to Example	Which Boston group issued propaganda urging American colonists to resent British colonial policy?				
Example to Idea		How did John Locke influence the Declaration of Independence?			
Evaluation			Did the Articles of Confederation establish an effective tax collection system? Why or why not?		

ThinkTrix: Tools to Teach 7 Essential Thinking Skills
Kagan Publishing • (800) 933-2667 • www.KaganOnline.com

ThinkTrix
Primary Social Studies Teacher Sample

Directions: Students and teacher may build a ThinkTrix model together.

	Families	Homes	Celebrations	Occupations	Education	Transportation	Rules and Laws
Recall	How many people are in your family?	Where do you live?	What holiday is celebrated on February 14th?	What is your mother's occupation?	What is the name of your school?	Name two kinds of transportation.	State one school rule.
Cause & Effect	What might happen if your mom had a new baby?	How might your home change if you lived in a rural area?	What decorations might you put up if you wanted to celebrate Hanukkah?	What might happen if we didn't have police officers?	How would your life change if you couldn't read?	How could you get to school if you missed the bus?	Why are school rules important?
Similarities	How is your family like _____'s family?	How is your home the same as _____'s home?	What holidays do all of the children in your class celebrate?	How are the jobs of a fireman and police officers the same?	How is your school like…?	What is the same about trains and subways?	How are the rules for home and school the same?
Differences	How is your family different from _____'s family?	How is your home different from _____'s home?	Tell how the Christopher Columbus ships differed from the Mayflower.	How are their jobs different?	How are the two schools different?	How are taxis and carpools different?	How are the rules for home and school different?
Example to Idea	What kinds of changes might occur in families?	Draw some examples of different kinds of homes.	Give some examples of family holidays.	What are some examples of community helpers?	Name some things you study in school.	Name as many forms of transportation as you can.	Name some responsibilities of a good citizen.
Idea to Example	What word do you think best describes your family?	What is the most important characteristic of all homes?	What kind of holiday is the 4th of July?	What could you conclude about a teacher, a nurse, and a librarian?	What is the main purpose of school?	How is a ferry an example of commuter transportation?	What one word would you use to describe our country?
Evaluation	Do you agree that all families are the same? Why? Why not?	Should all people live in the same type of home? Why? Why not?	Do you feel that there should be some new holidays? What would you celebrate?	Would you rather be a _____ or a _____? Why?	What do you like about school? Dislike?	Do you agree that cars are the safest way to travel? Why or why not?	What is the most important symbol of our country? Why?

Source: Nancy Koza

ThinkTrix Matrix
Art

The framework of thinking may be visualized as a matrix with one axis representing the focal points, and the other axis representing the thinking types, or mind actions, involved. This framework is useful for reminding teachers and students of questions to ask and types of responses to make. The focal points below are examples of what is appropriate for art and may be changed depending on content area or learning objective.

Focal Points

Thinking Types	1) Color	2) Line	3) Repetition	4) Focal Point	5) Shape	6) Texture	7) Pattern	8) Space
a) Recall								
b) Cause and Effect								
c) Similarity								
d) Difference								
e) Idea to Example								
f) Example to Idea								
g) Evaluation								

ThinkTrix: Tools to Teach 7 Essential Thinking Skills
Kagan Publishing • (800) 933-2667 • www.KaganOnline.com

ThinkTrix Matrix
Music

The framework of thinking may be visualized as a matrix with one axis representing the focal points, and the other axis representing the thinking types, or mind actions, involved. This framework is useful for reminding teachers and students of questions to ask and types of responses to make. The focal points below are examples of what is appropriate for one aspect of music and may be changed depending on content area or learning objective.

Focal Points

Thinking Types	1) Genre	2) Era	3) Composition	4) Style	5) Composers	6) Musicians	7) Instruments	8) Instruction
a) Recall								
b) Cause and Effect								
c) Similarity								
d) Difference								
e) Idea to Example								
f) Example to Idea								
g) Evaluation								

Chapter 8

ThinkTrix Tools

ThinkTrix Tools

Descriptions

The teacher can have a powerful effect on the understanding of the seven thinking types by showing the appropriate icons as the classroom conversation proceeds. This can be done by holding up the thinking type representing the question being asked or the conversation resulting from the question. This can also be accomplished by the teacher holding, wearing, or displaying a wheel with the types and a movable pointer or pointers. If the icon cards are magnetized, they can be conveniently placed to allow access for teacher or students. Of course, the kinesthetic learning can be enhanced if each student has pinch cards or a ThinkTrix wheel to manipulate as the discussion proceeds.

Crucial to the success of shared metacognition in the classroom are several tools for use by the teacher and the students. Following are the description of the tools, their purposes, and how to use them.

Thinking Types Posters

These seven Thinking Types Posters, if enlarged, can be seen from any part of the classroom. Their purpose is to be a constant reminder to the teacher and students of the types of thinking, or mind actions. Both teacher and students can create, respond to, and analyze questions, answers, and text by referring to the posters as memory cues. Each poster has the symbol/icon, the word name of the type, and sometimes words meant to define the type. See pages 156–169 for blacklines.

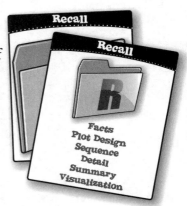

Handheld Thinking Wheel

The Handheld Thinking Wheel reminds students of the thinking types. The symbols stand alone on the wheel. Use the wheels when the students have an in-depth understanding of ThinkTrix. They are particularly useful as every-student-response tools when you ask students to create, respond to, and classify questions, responses, and text. Students move the arrow indicator to focus on the mind action. See page 170 for blackline.

Spinner Wheel

The Spinner Wheel encourages spontaneous interaction among students. Use it with RoundRobin, Think-Pair-Share, [spin/think/pair/share], and other cooperative structures. One student spins the arrow. The conversation or interaction begins when the arrow rests on an icon, a question is asked, and the thinking type classification is verified. The context is predetermined, but the departure point for thinking is not indicated. See page 170 for blackline.

Mind Actions Wheel

The Mind Actions Wheel is a one-dimensional wheel larger than the Handheld Thinking Wheel and the Spinner Wheel. All seven icons of the thinking types are displayed visibly to the class around the wheel. Move the arrow to the type of thinking when engaging in the question or the response. Students can lead the class using the wheel, also. See page 171 for blackline.

Double ThinkTrix Wheel

The two-dimensional WheelTrix is designed concentrically so that the outer orbit contains departure, or focal points, and the inner, revolving wheel contains the seven thinking types. The student rotates the inner wheel to a place adjacent to the desired departure point and rotates the pointer indicator to the juxtaposition of the thinking type and the departure point. As with the other handheld wheels, students craft questions, conversation follows, and questions and discussion can be analyzed metacognitively. See pages 172–173 for blacklines.

ThinkTrix Cubes or Die

ThinkTrix mind actions can be represented on a six sided cube or a die. The similarity and difference types are placed together on one side. The students use the ThinkTrix Cube or Die to create or respond to questions and responses. As with most of the ThinkTrix tools, they are best used in small group cooperative structures. See page 175 for blackline.

Movable Matrix ThinkTrix Cards

The Movable Matrix ThinkTrix Cards are two sets of cards that contain the thinking type icons on one set and the departure points for the content area on the other set. Students individually or in cooperative groups can match mind actions to departure points and create questions for discussion, cognitive mapping, or writing. Individually, they can follow conversation or text, **typing** the thinking. See page 176 for blackline.

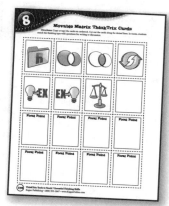

ThinkLink Prototype Cards

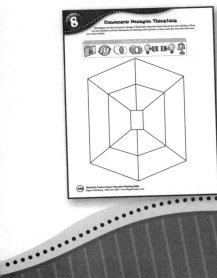

With the students, select ThinkLink Prototype Cards of various shapes or designs to post within sight. Students use these as a reference for creating visual representations of their thinking. Each map design or ThinkLink shape corresponds to one or more thinking types. There is no absolute design for a given thinking type, though some are more fitting to a mind action than others. See pages 186–200 for blacklines and examples.

ThinkTrix Pinch Strips

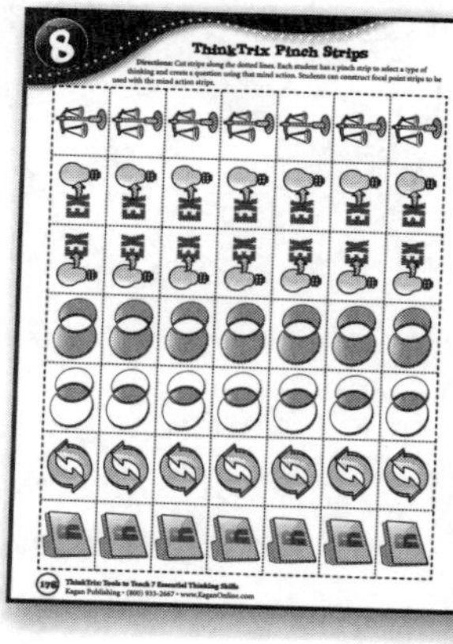

Each student has a pinch strip with the seven icons. They use the strip to select a type of thinking and create a question; or to indicate and show what type, or types, of thinking/questioning they are doing, hearing, or reading. The strips can be raised up in classroom discussion after Think Time so the teacher and students can check for their metacognitive understanding. This "every-student-response tool" is used to generate thought and a further understanding of how the mind works. The strips can be used in cooperative groups to increase the response and engagement. See page 178 for blackline.

ThinkTrix Cooperative Game Board

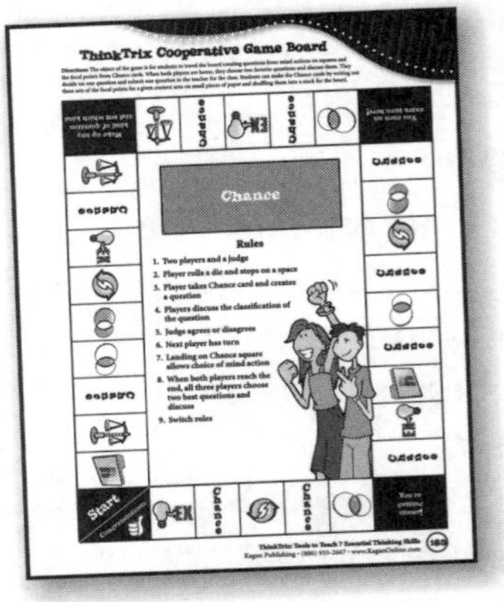

Rules of the Game: A student rolls the die and moves to the square. If the square is a mind action, a chance card is selected. These cards contain focal points. The student then crafts a question from this intersection and asks for confirmation from a teammate/friendly competitor. If agreement is reached on the classification, the piece stays and the partner rolls the die and follows the same procedure. If a player lands on a chance square, a card is selected and he or she can choose a mind action and move to the next square containing this thinking type. When both reach the end of the board, they select two favorite questions and discuss them. The game is best played with a list of common reference points form the content area—a context list. See page 183 for blackline.

Two-Sided ThinkTrix Discussion Board

The Two-Sided ThinkTrix Discussion Board allows students sitting opposite each other to see the matrix in the same way. Each student in the pair has board markers to place upon the intersection that classifies the question being asked or the response being given. The student can place the marker on the cell when asking or responding to a question. When the response or question requires thinking of more than one type, as is often the case with evaluation questions, more than one marker can be placed. Discussion of the reasons for the classifications can precede the answering and discussion of the question, but as in all ThinkTrix activities, the metacognitive analysis of the thinking is of secondary importance to a meaningful discussion. This tool can be used with two students on each side of the board as well. In concert with the Discussion Boards, a list of contexts is crucial to the flow of the discussion, since the connecting of phenomena, ideas, stories, and events is essential to the learning experience. See pages 129–130, 133, 140, 145, and 182, for blacklines.

Problem-Solving Flowchart

Developed Jointly with Dr. George Eley

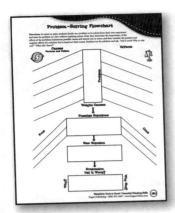

The Problem-Solving Flowchart is designed to give a structured cognitive path to problem solving. The first step is to state the problem cleanly with no implied cause. Secondly, brainstorm the possible causes, watching for hidden causes. Then select the most likely cause(s) and decide on a solution based on these causes. Predict the positive and negative effects of the proposed solution. Try a solution and evaluate the results. What have you learned? This cognitive path consistently practiced and understood through ThinkTrix will be a companion in life as well as in school. See page 181 for blackline.

ThinkTrix Wall Chart

The ThinkTrix Wall Chart contains the letter and numeral code for each intersecting cell of the matrix. This facilitates discussion by allowing teacher and students to refer to a cell when classifying thinking or questions. See pages 84 and 177 for blacklines.

Sample Question Cards

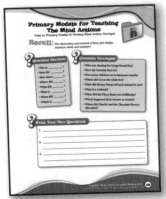

Use Sample Question Cards when the students, particularly primary, are first learning the meaning of the mind actions. These can be small, enlarged for the wall, or placed on a Question Starter Chart, but eventually removed or masked to avoid over reliance on them. Students have attained metacognitive understanding when they no longer need to see sample questions. See pages 59–65 for blacklines.

Thinking Types Poster
(Symbols)

Directions: Copy the poster and place on the wall in the classroom. Use as a reminder of thinking types/ mind actions for both students and the teacher.

Recall

Directions: Copy the poster and place on the wall in the classroom. Use as a reminder of thinking types/ mind actions for both students and the teacher.

Cause and Effect

Thinking Types Poster
(Symbols)

Directions: Copy the poster and place on the wall in the classroom. Use as a reminder of thinking types/ mind actions for both students and the teacher.

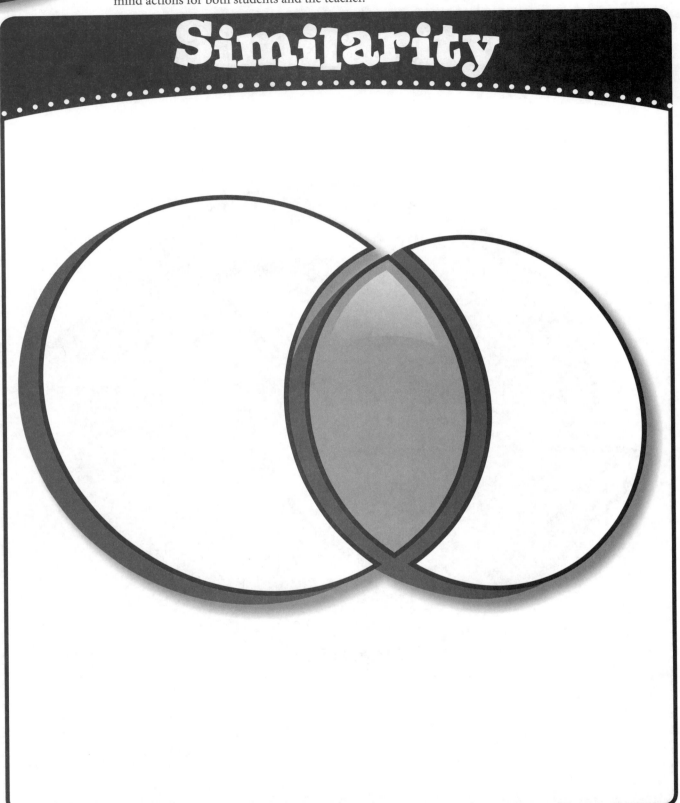

Similarity

ThinkTrix: Tools to Teach 7 Essential Thinking Skills
Kagan Publishing • (800) 933-2667 • www.KaganOnline.com

Directions: Copy the poster and place on the wall in the classroom. Use as a reminder of thinking types/ mind actions for both students and the teacher.

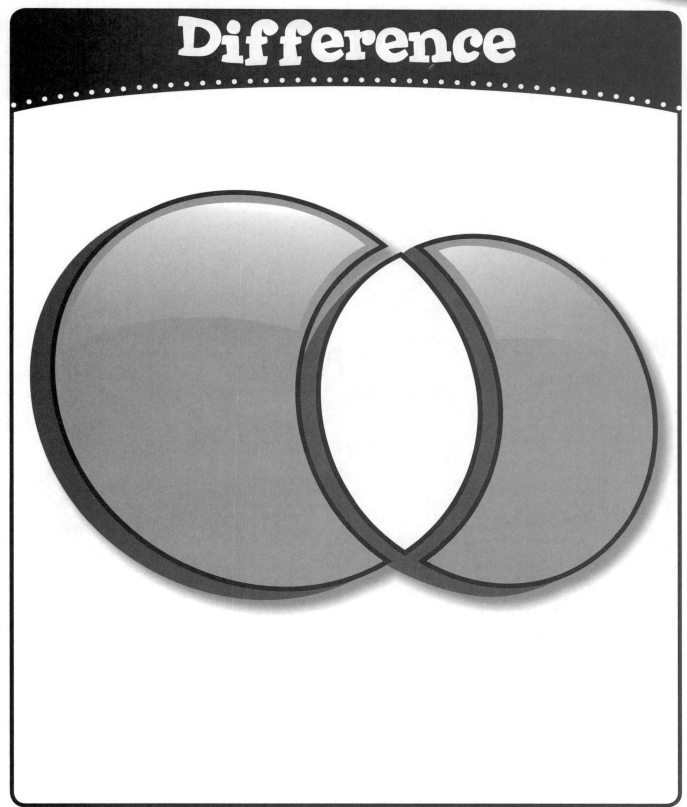

Difference

Thinking Types Poster
(Symbols)

Directions: Copy the poster and place on the wall in the classroom. Use as a reminder of thinking types/ mind actions for both students and the teacher.

Idea to Example

ThinkTrix: Tools to Teach 7 Essential Thinking Skills
Kagan Publishing • (800) 933-2667 • www.KaganOnline.com

Directions: Copy the poster and place on the wall in the classroom. Use as a reminder of thinking types/ mind actions for both students and the teacher.

Example to Idea

Thinking Types Poster
(Symbols)

Directions: Copy the poster and place on the wall in the classroom. Use as a reminder of thinking types/ mind actions for both students and the teacher.

Evaluation

ThinkTrix: Tools to Teach 7 Essential Thinking Skills
Kagan Publishing • (800) 933-2667 • www.KaganOnline.com

Thinking Types Poster
(Detailed)

Directions: Copy the poster and place on the wall in the classroom. Use as a reminder of thinking types/ mind actions for both students and the teacher.

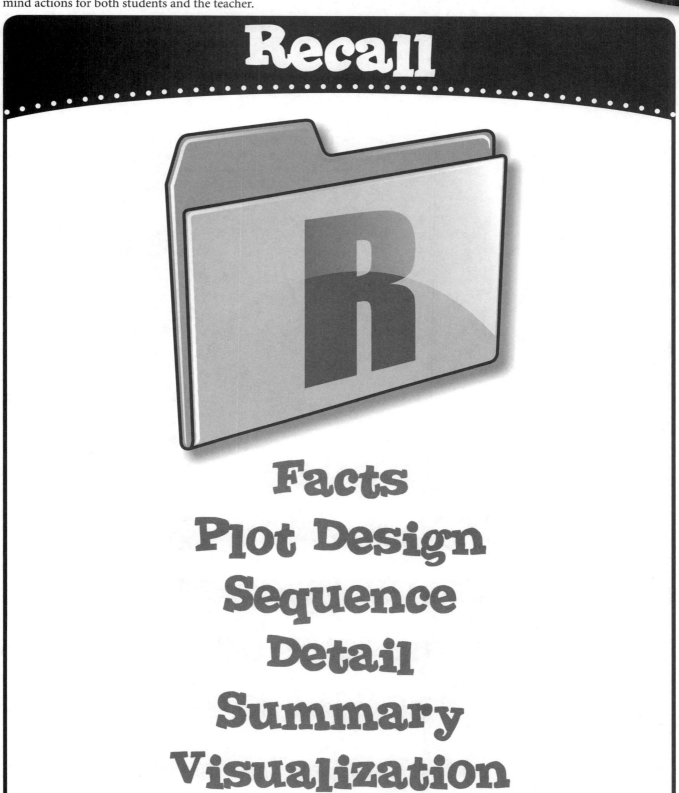

Recall

Facts
Plot Design
Sequence
Detail
Summary
Visualization

Thinking Types Poster
(Detailed)

Directions: Copy the poster and place on the wall in the classroom. Use as a reminder of thinking types/mind actions for both students and the teacher.

Cause and Effect

Cause
Effect/Result
Consequence
Inference
Prediction
Hypothesis

ThinkTrix: Tools to Teach 7 Essential Thinking Skills
Kagan Publishing • (800) 933-2667 • www.KaganOnline.com

Directions: Copy the poster and place on the wall in the classroom. Use as a reminder of thinking types/ mind actions for both students and the teacher.

Similarity

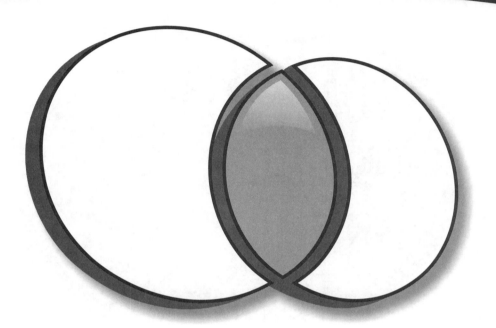

Analogy
Ratio
Comparison
Intersection

Directions: Copy the poster and place on the wall in the classroom. Use as a reminder of thinking types/mind actions for both students and the teacher.

Difference

Contrast
Distinction
Discrimination
Differentiation

ThinkTrix: Tools to Teach 7 Essential Thinking Skills
Kagan Publishing • (800) 933-2667 • www.KaganOnline.com

Thinking Types Poster
(Detailed)

Directions: Copy the poster and place on the wall in the classroom. Use as a reminder of thinking types/ mind actions for both students and the teacher.

Idea to Example

Analogy
Categorization
Deduction

Thinking Types Poster
(Detailed)

Directions: Copy the poster and place on the wall in the classroom. Use as a reminder of thinking types/ mind actions for both students and the teacher.

Example to Idea

Classification
Induction
Conclusion
Generalization
Finding Essence

ThinkTrix: Tools to Teach 7 Essential Thinking Skills
Kagan Publishing • (800) 933-2667 • www.KaganOnline.com

Directions: Copy the poster and place on the wall in the classroom. Use as a reminder of thinking types/mind actions for both students and the teacher.

Evaluation

Value
Ethics
Judgment
Rating

Handheld Thinking Wheel
and Spinner Wheel

Directions: Cut out the wheel and arrow. Use a brad to attach the arrow to the center of the wheel. Students move the arrow to the thinking type while asking or responding to a question. Laminate the wheel for durability.

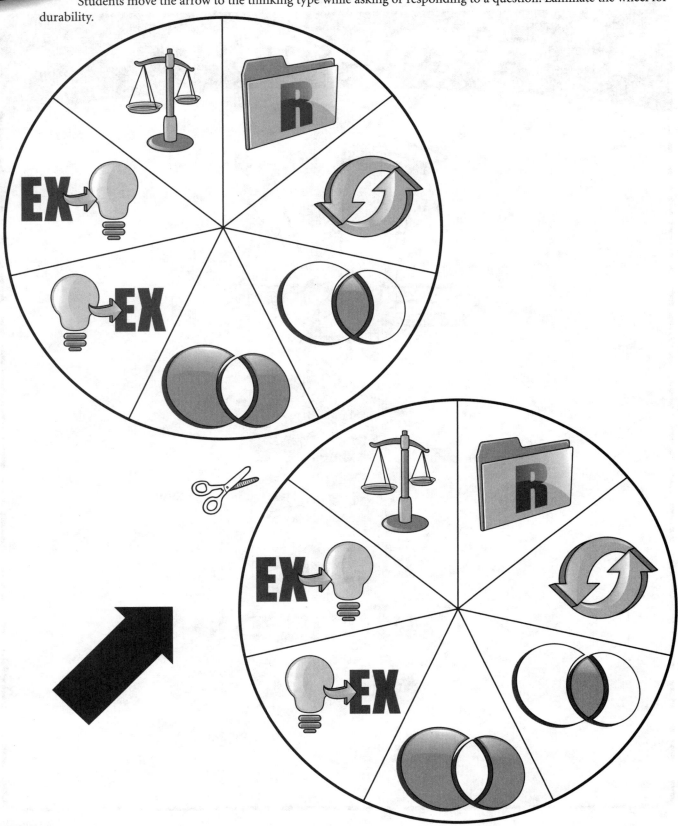

ThinkTrix: Tools to Teach 7 Essential Thinking Skills
Kagan Publishing • (800) 933-2667 • www.KaganOnline.com

Mind Actions Wheel

Directions: Cut out the wheel and arrow. Use a brad to attach the arrow to the center of the wheel. Students move the arrow to the thinking type while asking or responding to a question. Laminate the wheel for durability.

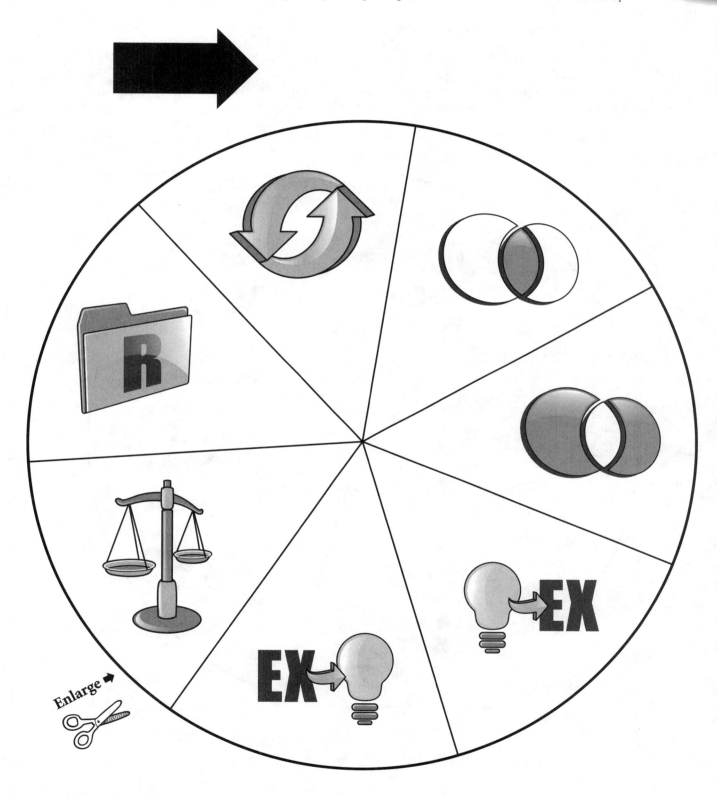

Enlarge ➜

Double ThinkTrix Wheel
Top Wheel

Directions

1. Copy the top and bottom Double ThinkTrix wheels onto construction paper. Cut out each wheel.
2. Punch a hole in the center of the two wheels and attach a brad through the holes, not too tight, so wheels can spin.
3. Use the bottom wheel (facing page) to fill in the focal points that work with your lesson.
4. **Optional:** Laminate the wheel for durability.

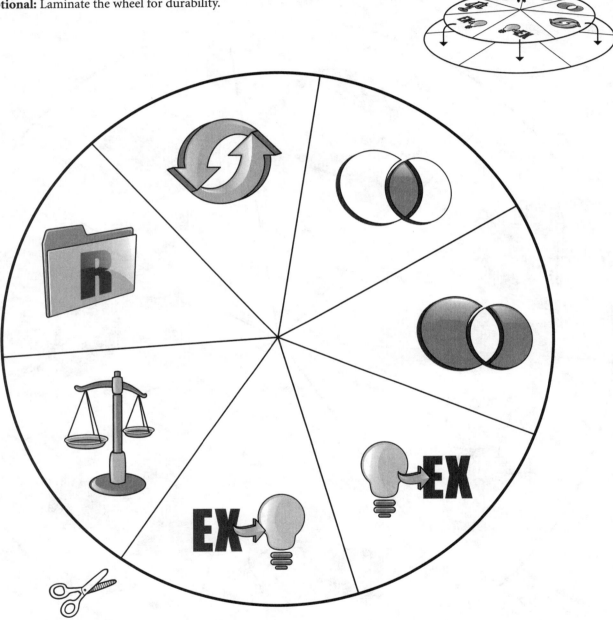

Double ThinkTrix Wheel
Bottom Wheel

Directions: Fill in a focal point in each cell. See the sample of the Language Arts Double ThinkTrix Wheel on the next page.

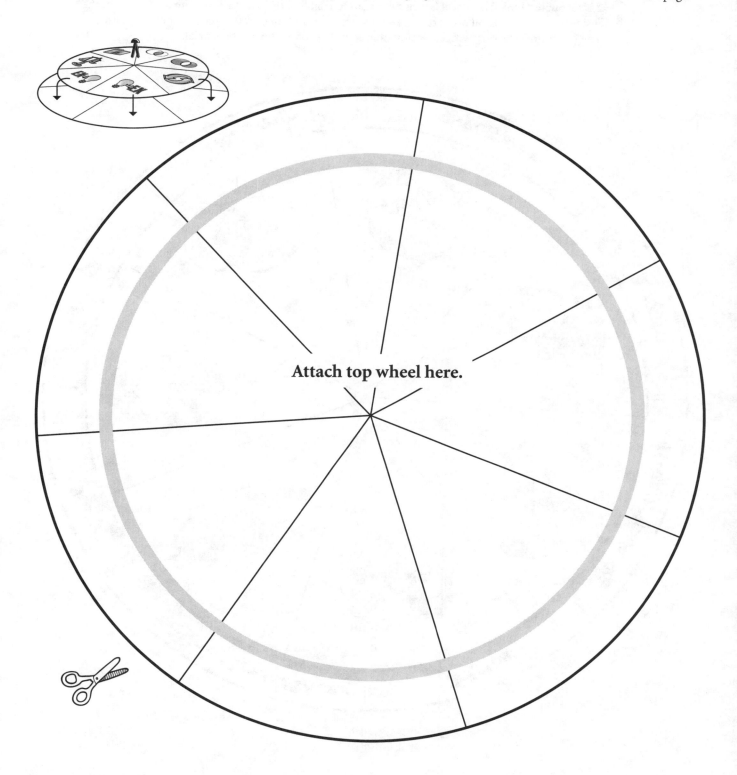

Attach top wheel here.

Double ThinkTrix Wheel
Language Arts Wheel Sample

This Double ThinkTrix Wheel is a circular matrix, enabling the user to match up an icon from the inside wheel with a focal point on the outer wheel rim, and then craft a question or a response. The outer rim cells vary with subject matter. A wall list of contexts is beneficial.

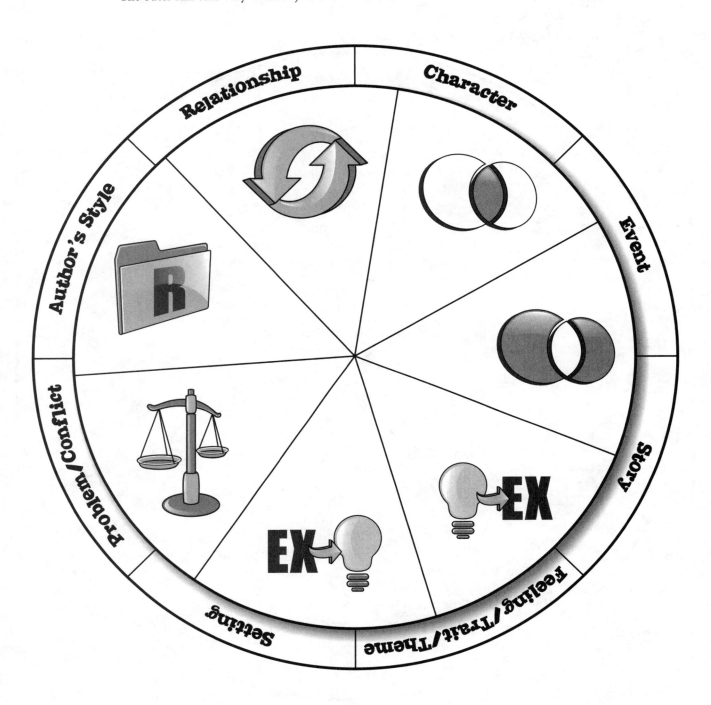

ThinkTrix: Tools to Teach 7 Essential Thinking Skills
Kagan Publishing • (800) 933-2667 • www.KaganOnline.com

ThinkTrix Cubes/ThinkTrix Dice

Directions: Copy the cube pattern on cardstock. Cut out, fold, and tape together to form a cube. ThinkTrix can be placed on all six sides of a cube, **Similarity** and **Difference** occupying one side. The cubes can be of any size, even small enough to be used like dice. Cube cues lend the element of surprise for crafting questions, and when other cubes contain focal points, they become a rolling matrix. Use as a die for metacognitive thinking games and activities.

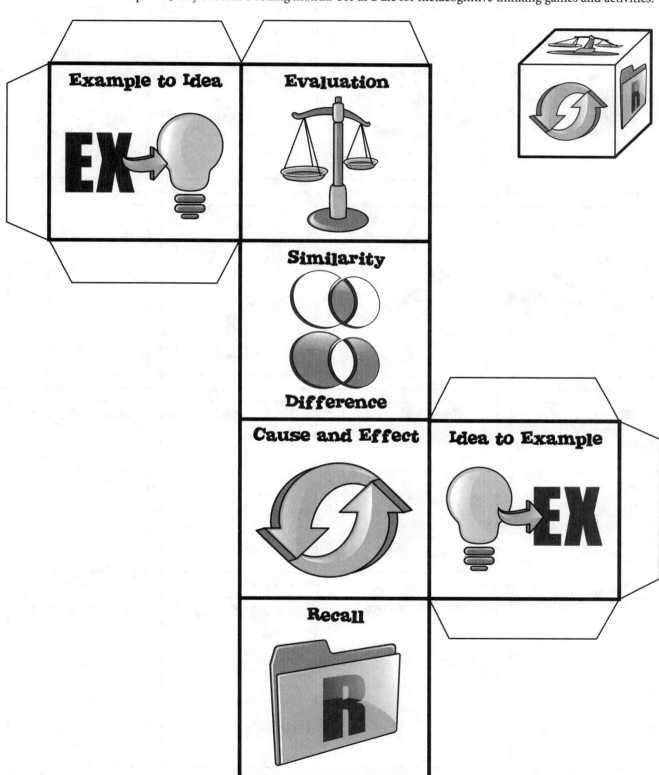

Movable Matrix ThinkTrix Cards

Directions: Copy or tape the cards on cardstock. Cut out the cards along the dotted lines. In teams, students match the thinking type with questions for writing or discussion.

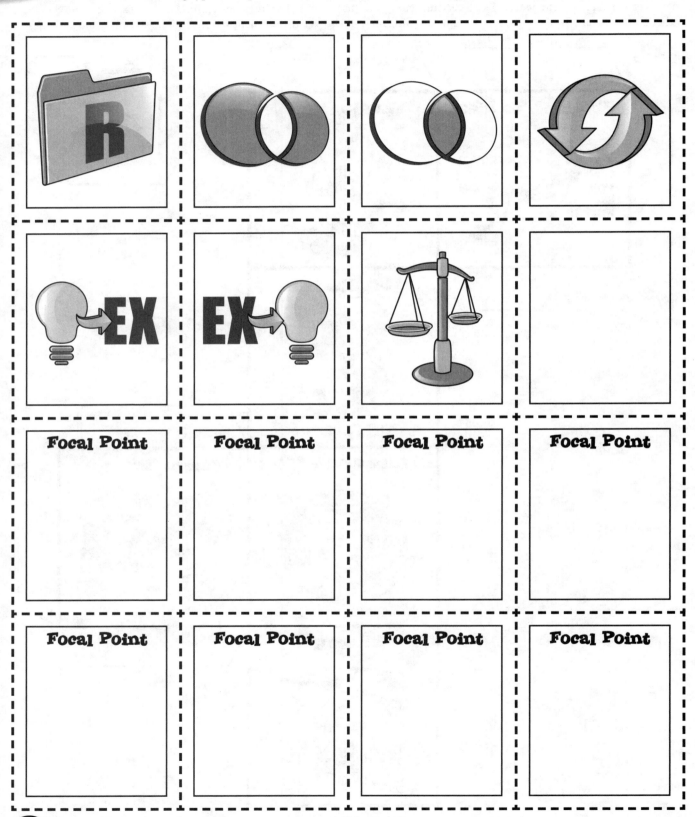

Focal Point

Focal Point

Focal Point

Focal Point

Focal Point

Focal Point

Focal Point

Focal Point

ThinkTrix: Tools to Teach 7 Essential Thinking Skills
Kagan Publishing • (800) 933-2667 • www.KaganOnline.com

ThinkTrix Wall Chart

Directions: Using this visible, cell-coded ThinkTrix Wall Chart, students and teachers can refer to the cell designations to create or classify questions or text. Enlarge for wall use.

Focal Points

Subject	1)	2)	3)	4)	5)	6)	7)	8)
a) Recall	1a	2a	3a	4a	5a	6a	7a	8a
b) Cause and Effect	1b	2b	3b	4b	5b	6b	7b	8b
c) Similarity	1c	2c	3c	4c	5c	6c	7c	8c
d) Difference	1d	2d	3d	4d	5d	6d	7d	8d
e) Idea to Example	1e	2e	3e	4e	5e	6e	7e	8e
f) Example to Idea	1f	2f	3f	4f	5f	6f	7f	8f
g) Evaluation	1g	2g	3g	4g	5g	6g	7g	8g

Thinking Type

ThinkTrix Pinch Strips

Directions: Cut strips along the dotted lines. Each student has a pinch strip to select a type of thinking and create a question using that mind action. Students can construct focal point strips to be used with the mind action strips.

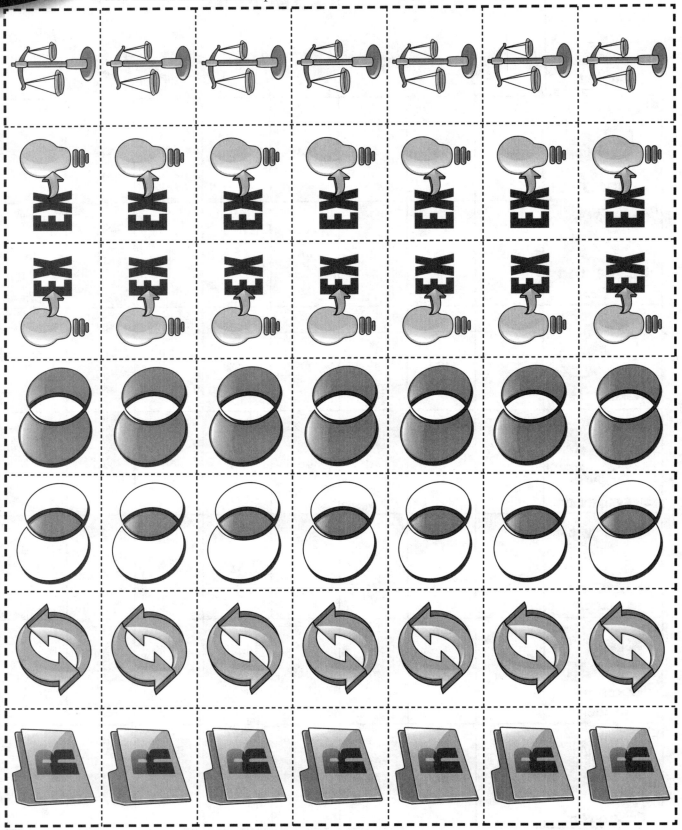

ThinkTrix: Tools to Teach 7 Essential Thinking Skills
Kagan Publishing • (800) 933-2667 • www.KaganOnline.com

Question Generator

Directions: Use the chart to create and analyze questions. The chart can be used by individuals or partners.

Name: _____

Topic or Assignment: _____

Mind Action	Type	Questions
	Recall	
	Cause and Effect	
	Similarity	
	Difference	
	Example to Idea	
	Idea to Example	
	Evaluate	

ThinkTrix Review Chart

Directions: Students use this chart by creating focal points and placing notes or questions in each cell; thinking about what they know by going from cell to cell.

Focal Points

	Recall	Cause and Effect	Similarity	Difference	Idea to Example	Example to Idea	Evaluation

ThinkTrix: Tools to Teach 7 Essential Thinking Skills
Kagan Publishing • (800) 933-2667 • www.KaganOnline.com

Problem-Solving Flowchart

Directions: In teams or pairs, students decide on a problem to be solved from their own experience and state the problem as a fact without implying causes. Next, they determine the importance of the effects of the problem; brainstorm possible causes and choose one or more, and then consider the positive and negative effects of a solution that is based on these causes. Students try the solution and ask, *"Did it work? Why or why not?" "What did I learn?"*

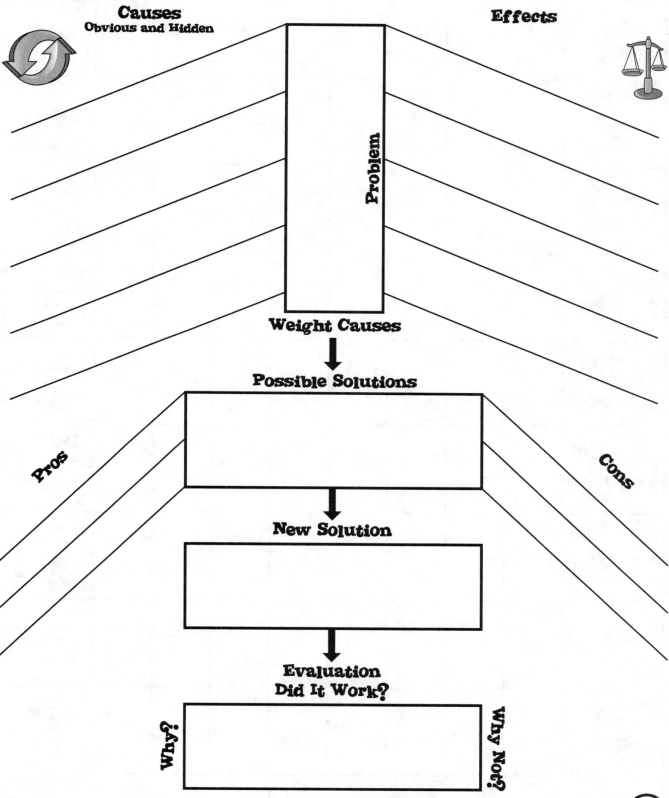

Causes
Obvious and Hidden

Effects

Problem

Weight Causes

Possible Solutions

Pros

Cons

New Solution

Evaluation
Did It Work?

Why?

Why Not?

Two-Sided ThinkTrix
Discussion Board Blank Template

Directions: Individually or in pairs, students sit on opposite sides of the board. Students on one side ask a question and place a marker on the cell(s) that prompted it. Students on the other side confirm or doubt the classification and try to answer. Discussion follows. Alternating back and forth, students on the other side frame a question and begin the process again. The focal points are written and placed on both sides of the board.

THINK TRIX								THINK TRIX
Recall								Recall
Cause and Effect								Cause and Effect
Similarity								Similarity
Difference								Difference
Idea to Example								Idea to Example
Example to Idea								Example to Idea
Evaluation								Evaluation
THINK TRIX								THINK TRIX

Source: Belinda Miller

ThinkTrix: Tools to Teach 7 Essential Thinking Skills
Kagan Publishing • (800) 933-2667 • www.KaganOnline.com

ThinkTrix Cooperative Game Board

Directions: The object of the game is for students to travel the board creating questions from mind actions on squares and the focal points from Chance cards. When both players are home, they choose two favorite questions and discuss them. They decide on one question and submit one question to the teacher for the class. Students can make the Chance cards by writing out three sets of the focal points for a given content area on small pieces of paper and shuffling them into a stack for the board.

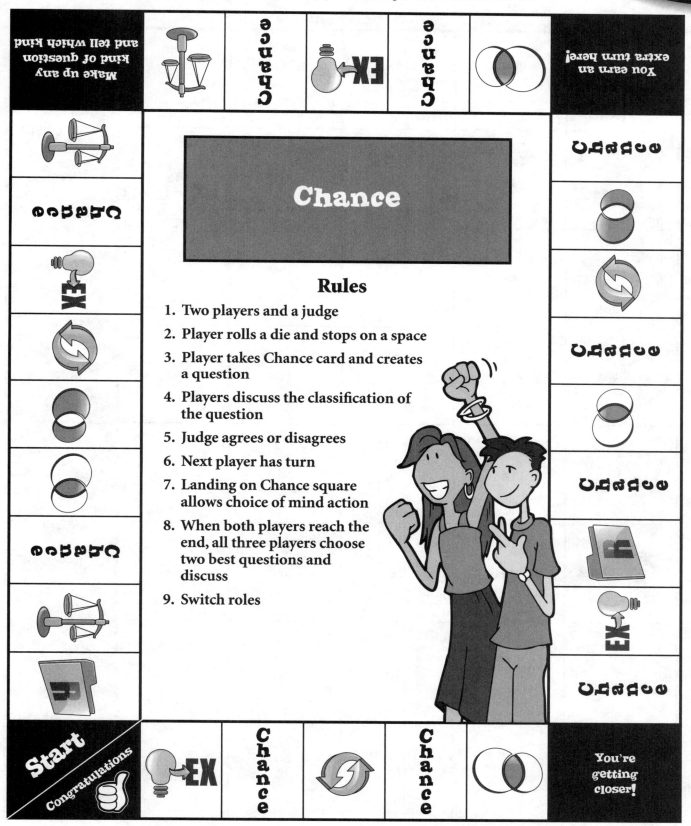

Chance

Rules

1. Two players and a judge
2. Player rolls a die and stops on a space
3. Player takes Chance card and creates a question
4. Players discuss the classification of the question
5. Judge agrees or disagrees
6. Next player has turn
7. Landing on Chance square allows choice of mind action
8. When both players reach the end, all three players choose two best questions and discuss
9. Switch roles

Thinking Matrix

Directions: Primary students use this ThinkTrix chart to make up and discuss questions. The words are used as reminders. Fewer focal points are helpful in making choices.

Focal Points

Thinking Types	1)	2)	3)	4)	
a)	1a	2a	3a	4a	**Recall**
b)	1b	2b	3b	4b	**Cause and Effect**
c)	1c	2c	3c	4c	**Similarity**
d)	1d	2d	3d	4d	**Difference**
e)	1e	2e	3e	4e	**Idea to Example**
f)	1f	2f	3f	4f	**Example to Idea**
g)	1g	2g	3g	4g	**Evaluation**

ThinkTrix: Tools to Teach 7 Essential Thinking Skills
Kagan Publishing • (800) 933-2667 • www.KaganOnline.com

Introduction to ThinkLinks
All Thought Has Shape

The ThinkLink graphic organizers that follow are only a sampling of the possible ways to make thought visible and to give students access to the geometry of the workings of their minds. Metacognition through ThinkTrix mind actions is enhanced by visible representation. ThinkLinks have been discussed throughout the pages of this book. In this section, we get into an in-depth presentation for a broader understanding of the thought process behind using ThinkLinks. The completed ThinkLinks in this section demonstrate only a few ways that students can think using ThinkTrix and ThinkLinks in tandem. The mind actions at the top of each sample page are highlighted to show how the thinking flowed in the completion of these ThinkLinks. Study these samples to develop for yourself an understanding of the thinking flow. The blank ThinkLink designs that are opposite the sample completed ThinkLink may be used in ways similar to those in the completed designs or in other ways using other mind actions. When students use the blank designs as blacklines, they may circle the mind action symbols at the top of each page to show their understanding of the flow of thought as they completed the ThinkLink. When they create their own designs, these or others they create, they can draw in the relevant mind action icons. The examples given here, many of which were originally created by students, are meant to give the teacher and students a start with visual metacognition, and are intended as a model and an incentive to students and teachers to develop their own designs and uses. They and others may be enlarged for display on the wall.

Introducing ThinkLinks to Students

Choose the ThinkLink shape or design that best fits the types of thinking you want to do. For instance, if you want to think about a theme or idea, such as conflict in literature/politics/science or any other area, the all-purpose **Concentric Wheel** works well. For multiple examples of a concept/theme/generalization/ phenomenon, the **Concentic Hexagon** fits.

To build a structure of knowledge by asking **Cause and Effect** questions in any content area, **Dangling Boxes** can contain the answers well. Character analysis can be made aptly visible by a **Character Web**.

To develop an answer to a complex question involving **Cause and Effect** reasoning and Similarity thinking, and to use the design as a blueprint for expository composition, the **Jellyfish** designs are perfect.

The **Venn** diagram is ideal for making any comparison in which **Similarity** and **Difference** are analyzed.

The **Scale of Justice** is designed to weigh positive and negative effects in order to evaluate the rightness or wrongness of an act or a decision. What is ethical or moral is often the question suited to this design.

These are a small sampling of the hundreds of shapes available that can be utilized to visually display ThinkTrix knowledge building. The point is that all thinking has one or more visual design(s) that not only display it, but help you to do the thinking. If one of the ThinkLinks available to you does not seem right, design your own shape. "Be a ThinkLink inventor!"

Concentric Wheel ThinkLink

Directions: Use this Concentric Wheel ThinkLink to generate ideas and connect your thinking. When you have finished, and have discussed your thinking with a partner or team, circle the icons that show how your mind worked.

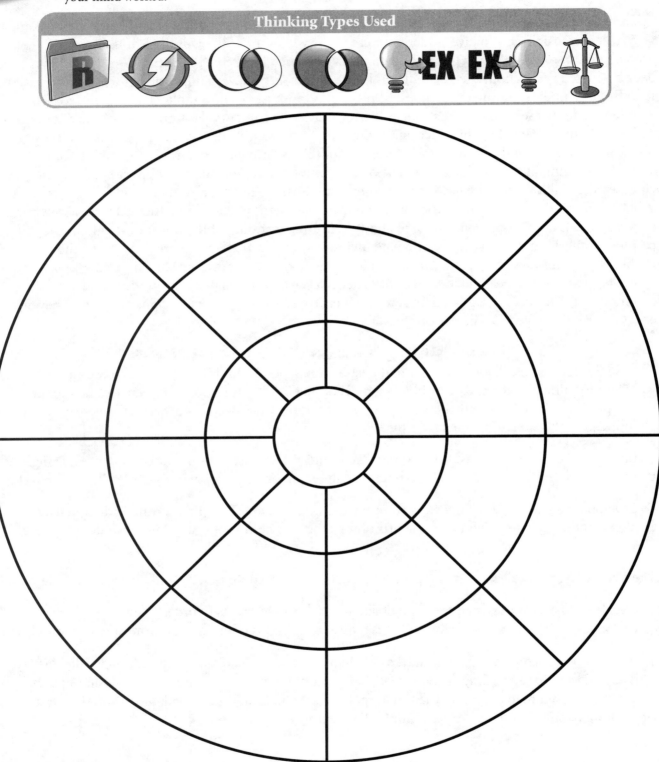

ThinkTrix: Tools to Teach 7 Essential Thinking Skills
Kagan Publishing • (800) 933-2667 • www.KaganOnline.com

Concentric Wheel ThinkLink Example

In this Concentric Wheel ThinkLink, students have identified the theme "Conflict" in the story. They then entered examples in the parallel orbit spots that show the two sources of each conflict, discussing each conflict. The thinking is from **Idea to Example**, once they have decided on a theme, but it is also **Cause and Effect** as they discussed the conflicts, and moved to **Similarity** and **Difference** as they discussed each example. If the theme choice arose from discussing the story, the process has begun from **Example to Idea**.

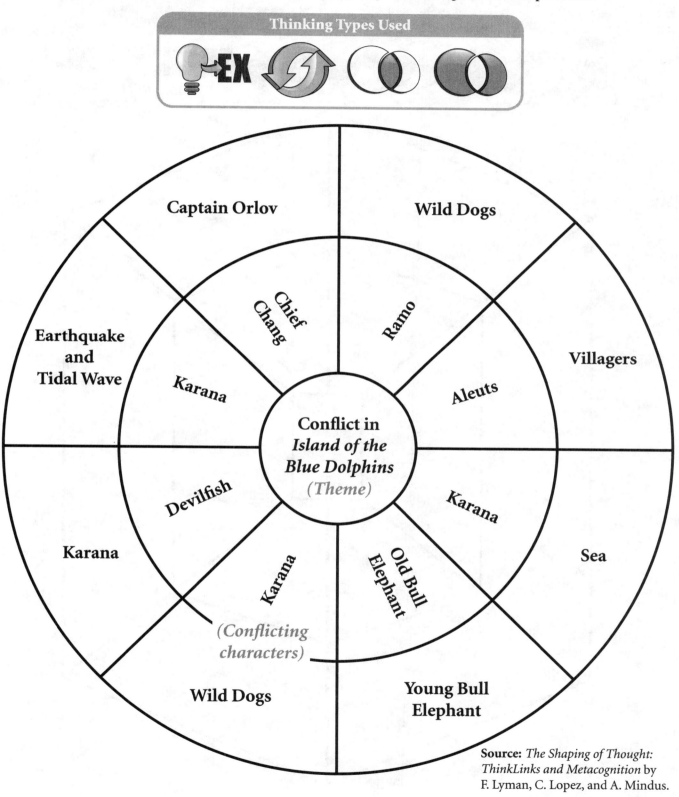

Source: *The Shaping of Thought: ThinkLinks and Metacognition* by F. Lyman, C. Lopez, and A. Mindus.

Concentric Hexagon ThinkLink

Directions: Use this Concentric Hexagon ThinkLink to generate ideas and connect your thinking. When you have finished, and have discussed your thinking with a partner or team, circle the icons that show how your mind worked.

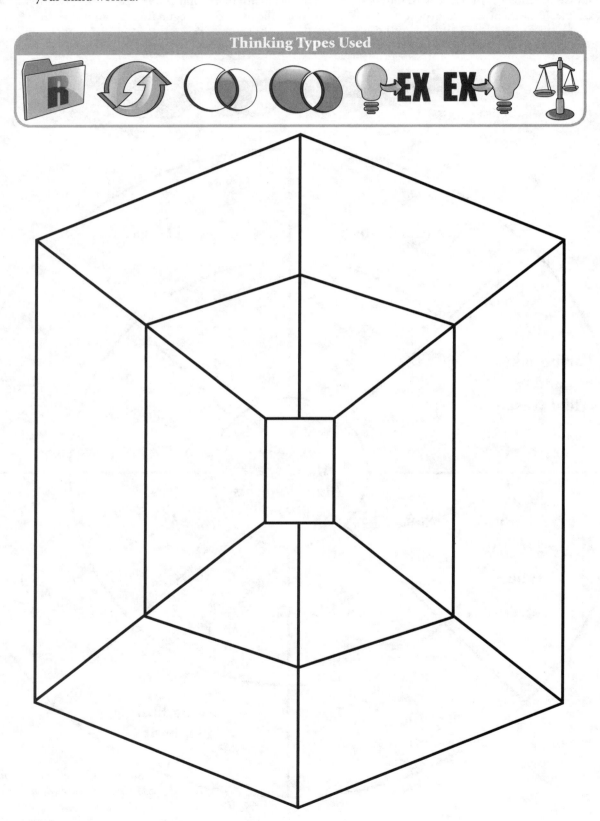

Concentric Hexagon ThinkLink Example

In this Concentric Hexagon ThinkLink, students have identified a theme "Helping" and chosen stories containing the theme. They then sought **Example to Idea** from the stories and charted examples from each story. Discussion of each example followed and the **Causes and Effect** of each example were discussed. **Similarity** and **Difference** among the examples can also be examined.

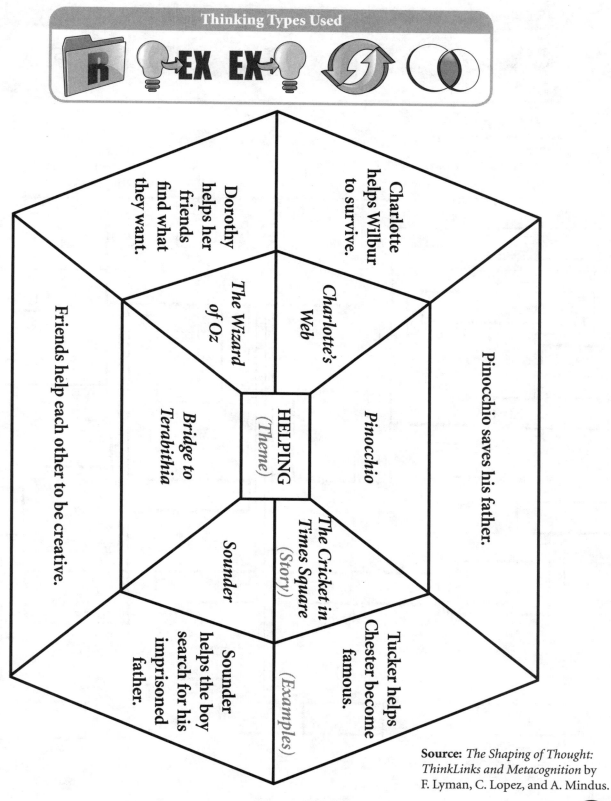

Source: *The Shaping of Thought: ThinkLinks and Metacognition* by F. Lyman, C. Lopez, and A. Mindus.

Dangling Boxes ThinkLink

Directions: Use this Dangling Boxes ThinkLink to generate ideas and connect your thinking. When you have finished, and have discussed your thinking with a partner or team, circle the icons that show how your mind worked.

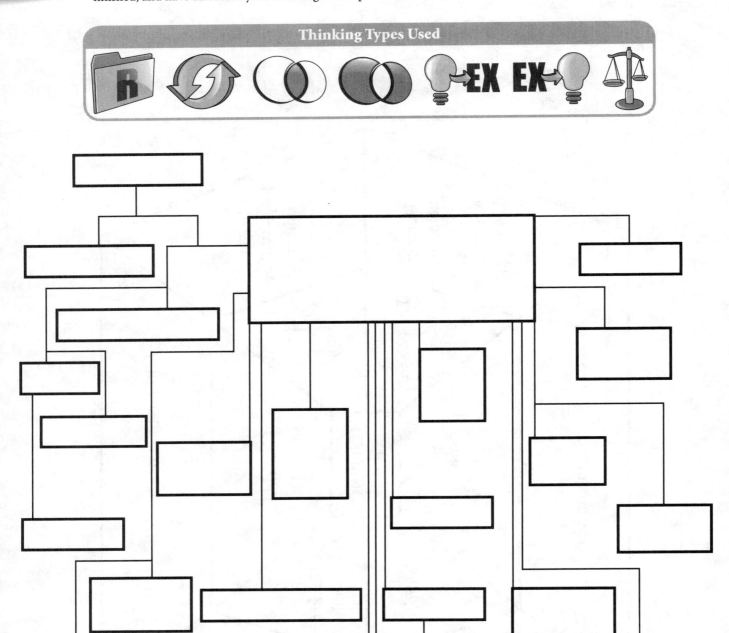

ThinkTrix: Tools to Teach 7 Essential Thinking Skills
Kagan Publishing • (800) 933-2667 • www.KaganOnline.com

Dangling Boxes ThinkLink Example

In this Dangling Boxes ThinkLink, students considered what the **causes** of building a friendship are by searching for examples in two similar stories and naming the examples. The thinking flowed from **Idea to Example to Idea. Cause and Effect** was used because each example was a cause of a friendship. The students have essentially constructed a theory of how to be a friend.

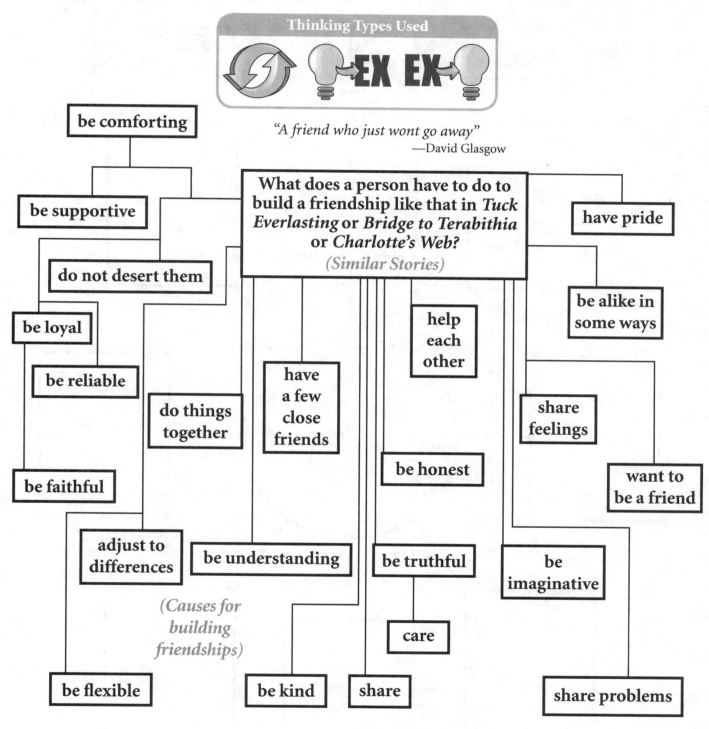

Thinking Types Used

EX EX

"A friend who just wont go away"
—David Glasgow

be comforting

be supportive

do not desert them

be loyal

be reliable

do things together

be faithful

What does a person have to do to build a friendship like that in *Tuck Everlasting* or *Bridge to Terabithia* or *Charlotte's Web*?
(Similar Stories)

have a few close friends

help each other

be honest

have pride

be alike in some ways

share feelings

want to be a friend

adjust to differences

be understanding

be truthful

be imaginative

(Causes for building friendships)

care

be flexible

be kind

share

share problems

Source: *The Shaping of Thought: ThinkLinks and Metacognition* by F. Lyman, C. Lopez, and A. Mindus.

Character Web ThinkLink

Directions: Use this Character Web ThinkLink to generate ideas and connect your thinking. When you have finished, and have discussed your thinking with a partner or team, circle the icons that show how your mind worked.

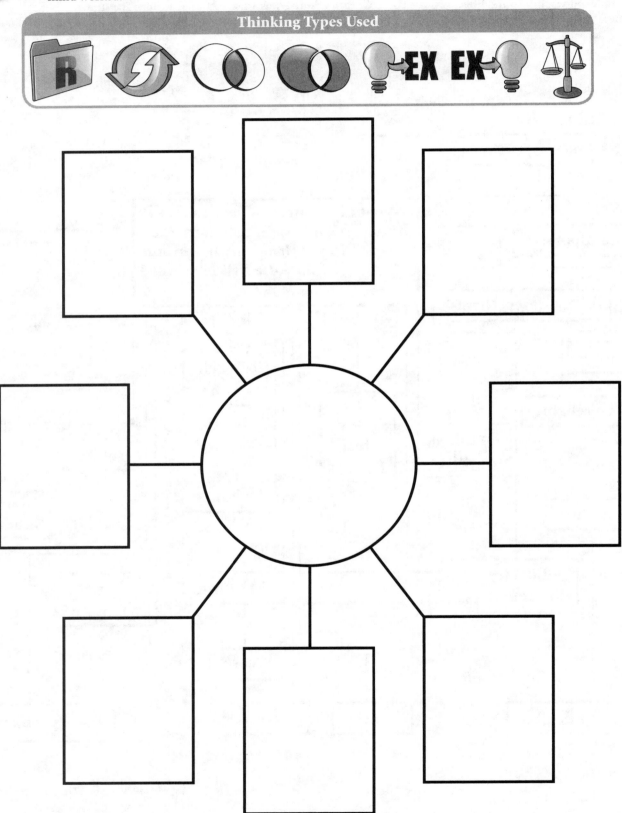

ThinkTrix: Tools to Teach 7 Essential Thinking Skills
Kagan Publishing • (800) 933-2667 • www.KaganOnline.com

Character Web ThinkLink Example

In this Character Web ThinkLink, students have identified emotions and character traits of Helen Keller and supported these ideas with examples. They discussed the examples and the effects on Helen's life. The thinking flowed from **Example to Idea** and **Idea to Example** and then to the effects of the events on Helen's life.

Thinking Types Used

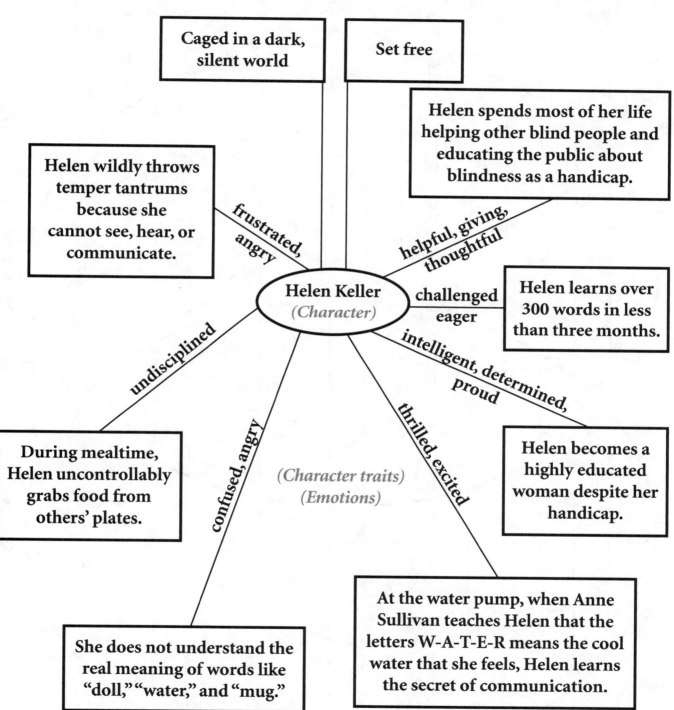

Caged in a dark, silent world

Set free

Helen wildly throws temper tantrums because she cannot see, hear, or communicate.

frustrated, angry

Helen spends most of her life helping other blind people and educating the public about blindness as a handicap.

helpful, giving, thoughtful

Helen Keller
(Character)

challenged eager

Helen learns over 300 words in less than three months.

undisciplined

intelligent, determined, proud

During mealtime, Helen uncontrollably grabs food from others' plates.

confused, angry

(Character traits)
(Emotions)

thrilled, excited

Helen becomes a highly educated woman despite her handicap.

She does not understand the real meaning of words like "doll," "water," and "mug."

At the water pump, when Anne Sullivan teaches Helen that the letters W-A-T-E-R means the cool water that she feels, Helen learns the secret of communication.

Source: *The Shaping of Thought: ThinkLinks and Metacognition* by F. Lyman, C. Lopez, and A. Mindus.

Venn ThinkLink

Directions: Use this Venn ThinkLink to generate ideas and connect your thinking. When you have finished, and have discussed your thinking with a partner or team, circle the icons that show how your mind worked.

Thinking Types Used

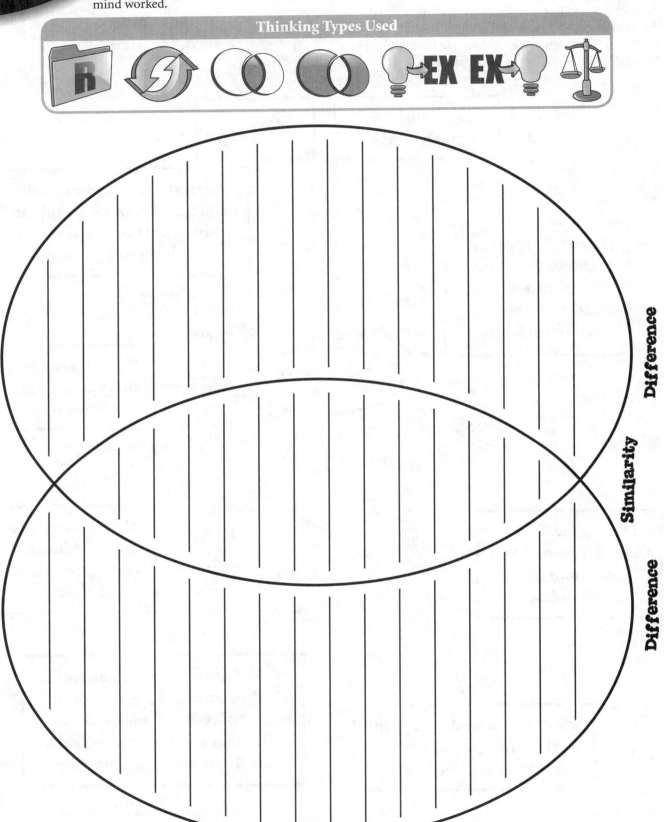

Difference

Similarity

Difference

ThinkTrix: Tools to Teach 7 Essential Thinking Skills
Kagan Publishing • (800) 933-2667 • www.KaganOnline.com

Venn ThinkLink Example

Directions: With this Venn ThinkLink, Social Studies students compared Abraham Lincoln and George Washington according to multiple aspects of their lives. As with all mapping of thought, **Recall** is a necessary mind action. Students have read biographies online of the two presidents and found and charted **Similarity** and **Difference** between them. This comparative analysis led to the question, discussed in pairs, of what are the qualities both men had in common that can be causes of their enormous influence on our lives today? The thinking then became **Cause and Effect** and **Evaluation**.

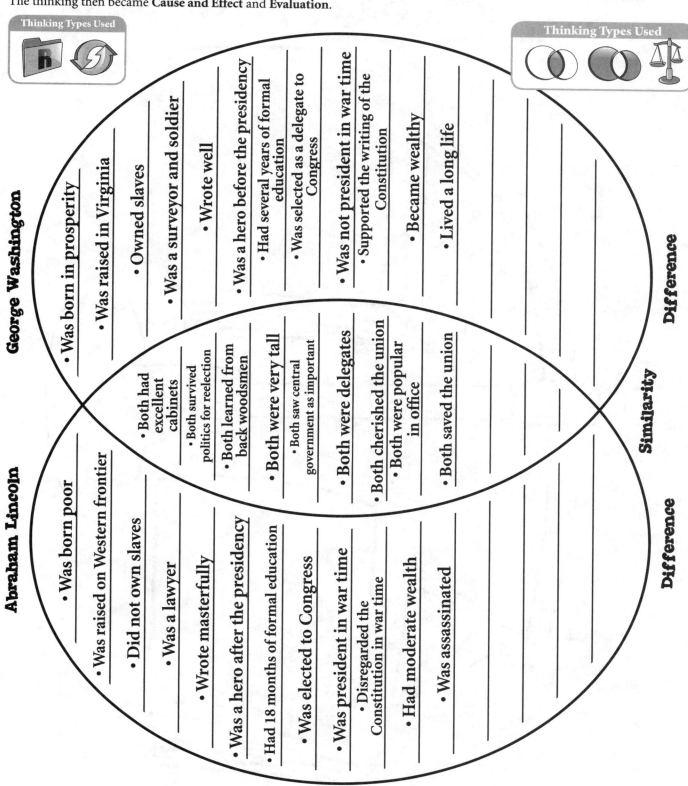

Thinking Types Used

Thinking Types Used

George Washington

- Was born in prosperity
- Was raised in Virginia
- Owned slaves
- Was a surveyor and soldier
- Wrote well
- Was a hero before the presidency
- Had several years of formal education
- Was selected as a delegate to Congress
- Was not president in war time
- Supported the writing of the Constitution
- Became wealthy
- Lived a long life

Difference

- Both had excellent cabinets
- Both survived politics for reelection
- Both learned from back woodsmen
- Both were very tall
- Both saw central government as important
- Both were delegates
- Both cherished the union
- Both were popular in office
- Both saved the union

Similarity

Abraham Lincoln

- Was born poor
- Was raised on Western frontier
- Did not own slaves
- Was a lawyer
- Wrote masterfully
- Was a hero after the presidency
- Had 18 months of formal education
- Was elected to Congress
- Was president in war time
- Disregarded the Constitution in war time
- Had moderate wealth
- Was assassinated

Difference

Scale of Justice ThinkLink

Directions: Use this Scale of Justice ThinkLink to generate ideas and connect your thinking. When you have finished, and have discussed your thinking with a partner or team, circle the icons that show how your mind worked.

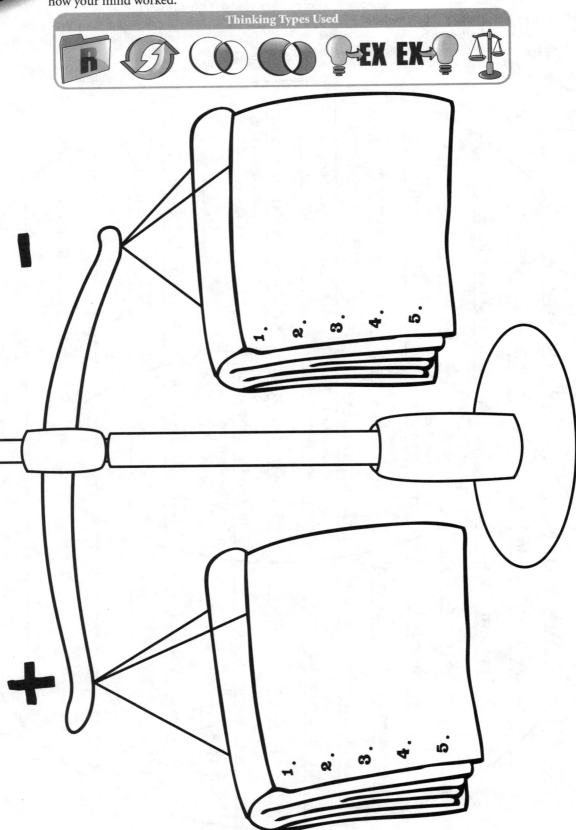

ThinkTrix: Tools to Teach 7 Essential Thinking Skills
Kagan Publishing • (800) 933-2667 • www.KaganOnline.com

Scale of Justice ThinkLink Example

Using the Scale of Justice ThinkLink, Sociology students used their experience to arrive at the effects of lying and telling the truth. Their thinking flowed from **Example to Ideas**. They then charted the ideas and tried to decide, in pair discussion, whether it is ever right to lie. The mind actions used were from **Cause and Effect** and **Evaluation**. They referred back to the original personal experience examples to support their evaluation, moving cognitively from **Idea to Example**.

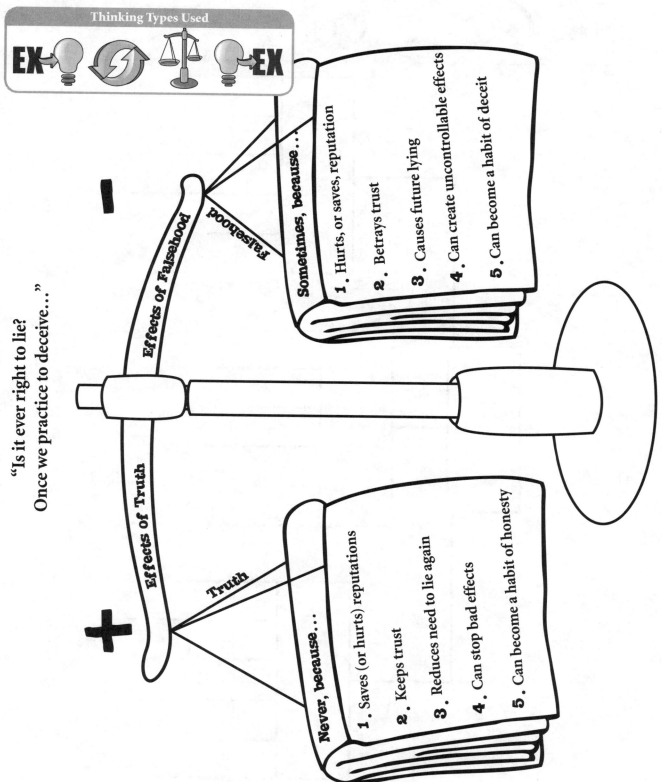

Thinking Types Used

"Is it ever right to lie? Once we practice to deceive…"

Effects of Falsehood — Falsehood

Sometimes, because…
1. Hurts, or saves, reputation
2. Betrays trust
3. Causes future lying
4. Can create uncontrollable effects
5. Can become a habit of deceit

Effects of Truth — Truth

Never, because…
1. Saves (or hurts) reputations
2. Keeps trust
3. Reduces need to lie again
4. Can stop bad effects
5. Can become a habit of honesty

Jellyfish ThinkLink

Directions: Use this Jellyfish ThinkLink to generate ideas and connect your thinking. When you have finished, and have discussed your thinking with a partner or team, circle the icons that show how your mind worked.

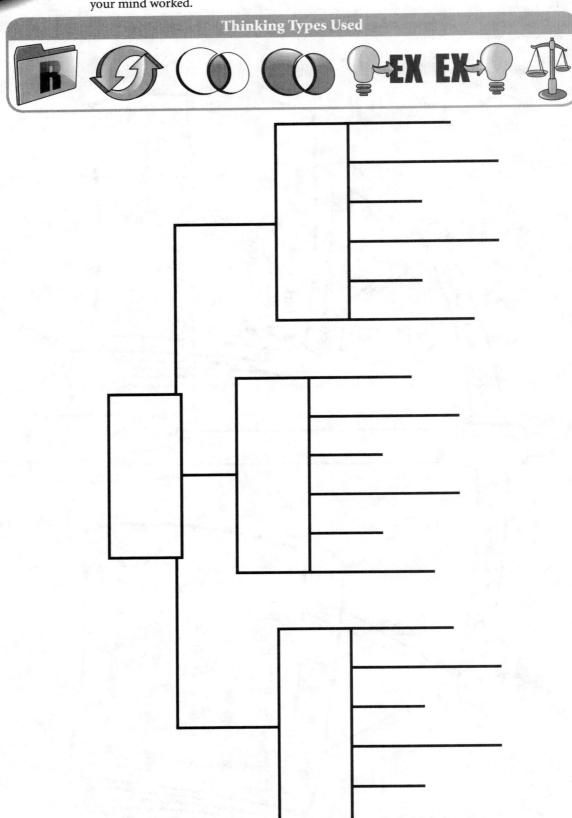

ThinkTrix: Tools to Teach 7 Essential Thinking Skills
Kagan Publishing • (800) 933-2667 • www.KaganOnline.com

Jellyfish ThinkLink
Character–Event Comparison Example

In the Jellyfish Character-Event Comparison ThinkLink, the students have found **Similarity** among three literary characters by examining the similar events in their lives. The descriptions of the events contain ideas such as "almost," "helped," and "changes," that are the ideas connecting the characters. The thinking flows from **Example to Idea** and ends with finding the **Similarity** among the ideas. Students have created an analogy.

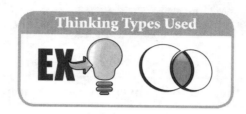

Thinking Types Used

Pinocchio *(Character)*	Cinderella *(Character)*	Cowardly Lion *(Character)*

He's almost swallowed. △

He's helped by a friend. ☆

He is frightened by a cat and fox. ○

He changes to a real boy. ▢

She's almost discovered. △

She's helped by a friend. ☆

She's frightened by her stepmother. ○

She changes into a princess. ▢

He's almost caught. △

He's helped by a friend. ☆

He's frightened by everyone. ○

He changes to a brave lion. ▢

(Similarities)

Source: *The Shaping of Thought: ThinkLinks and Metacognition* by F. Lyman, C. Lopez, and A. Mindus.

Jellyfish ThinkLink
Essay Blueprint Example

With the Jellyfish ThinkLink Essay Blueprint, the students have asked a complex **Cause and Effect** question. They then chose characters from literature as well as a friend of one of the students, all of whom helped another character change for the better. After thinking of the ways this helping occurred, they listed these on the strands and discussed **Similarity and Difference** among the ways. The second sample below illustrates how the students classified the events into ideas and found confirming examples from these and more stories. To use the thinking as a blueprint for an essay, the parts would be converted to paragraphs, with the concluding paragraph being the second ThinkLink.

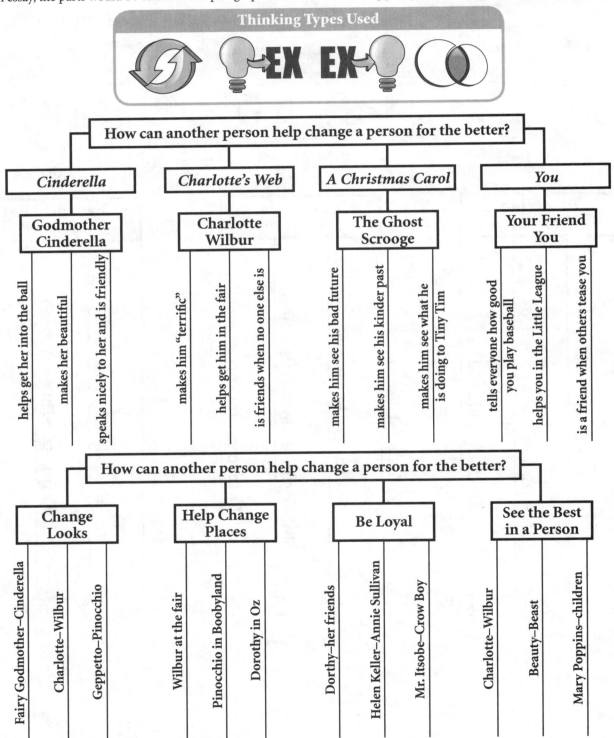

Source: *The Shaping of Thought: ThinkLinks and Metacognition* by F. Lyman, C. Lopez, and A. Mindus.

ThinkTrix: Tools to Teach 7 Essential Thinking Skills
Kagan Publishing • (800) 933-2667 • www.KaganOnline.com

ThinkTrix Glossary of Terms

- **Activity**—What students do and are focused upon within a learning structure.
- **Blueprint**—A ThinkLink used as an outline, or organizer, for written composition.
- **Clarity**—The state of mutual understanding that exists when a concept or topic being discussed has sufficient concrete referents.
- **Cognitive mapping**—Generic term for shaping of thought; synonymous in general with ThinkLinking.
- **Context lists**—Lists of classroom common references, usually topics, themes, areas of study, or common experiences such as books and film. These are reference points to make connections and they constitute a third dimension, or axis, of ThinkTrix, together with the mind actions and the focal points.
- **Cross–cultural heroism**—The aiding of people from a different ethnic or cultural backgrounds, within a threatening situation.
- **Cues**—Written, verbal, manipulative, and hand-signal reminders of what to do, how to think, and what is known.
- **Every–student–response**—A class room condition in which a maximum or high number of students are engaged and their engagement in the task is purposeful.
- **Example**—An event or object from which ideas can be derived or to which ideas can be attached.
- **Focal points**—The points of departure for thinking that make up one axis of the ThinkTrix grid. These vary according to the content area.
- **Idea**—Concept, theme, or generalization; an abstraction.
- **Instructional tool**—Any device, chart, comprehensive reminder, template, or list that facilitates classroom learning and teaching.
- **Known to unknown**—The direction of thinking that determines whether the thinking type/mind action should be classified as **Idea to Example** or **Example to Idea**. A classic example of how this works is the question: *"Is a whale a mammal?"* This is an **Example to Idea** question because we know what a whale is, but not what its class is. Hence, example (whale)(known) to idea (mammal)(unknown). Another example is when asking about character traits the thinking goes from examples/events (known) in the story to the general naming of a character trait (unknown). Hence, from **Example to Idea**.
- **Metacognition**—Knowing how you know; knowledge of the workings of the mind.
- **Metacognitive anchoring**—A translating process whereby the teacher and students can connect the fitting mind actions to a more abstractly worded thinking concept, such as hypothesis, inference, or summary. This process, consistently used by the teacher provides clarity as well as deepening the understanding of the more abstract concept.
- **Prompt**—Term referring to a question being asked or a task given in the classroom.
- **Prototype**—A format; a ThinkLink shape, form, or design coupled with the thinking type(s) and focal point involved; a blank model.

ThinkTrix Glossary of Terms *(continued)*

- **Question-response cues**—ThinkTrix thinking types displayed on the matrix or individually that can also be prompted verbally or with hand signals.
  - **Response prompts**—Questions or statements in various types of thinking designed to elicit responses.

- **Structure**—A scripted format within which to organize a learning activity and can be used with any content. Examples would be RoundRobin and Think-Pair-Share.

- **Theme**—A recurring idea; a "thread" running through a story or composition.

- **Theory making**—A process wherein students generalize to extract the key components of any phenomenon. This constructivist process is prompted by a questions such as, *"How do people learn?" "What makes a friendship?" "What causes conflict?"* The mind actions necessary are Idea to Example, Example to Idea, Similarity, and others.

- **ThinkLink**—A diagram of thinking, named by Tom Bruner, student friendly.

- **ThinkLink prototypes**—Different cognitive map designs placed in view to give students options for charting their thinking, using the mind actions.

- **ThinkLinking**—A strategy to visually shape thought.

- **ThinkTrix**—A matrix with thinking types on one axis and points of departure on the other axis; a basic and accessible metacognitive typology, named by Tom Payne.

- **Thought process**—Thinking that incorporates more than one thinking type; complex thinking such as problem solving, decision making, inquiring, and creating.

- **Trait**—A classification for an often-repeated pattern of behavior that may change, or evolve, or not.

- **Transactional cueing**—Signaling, usually by agreed upon hand gestures, between and among teachers and students, to indicate activity shift or actions of the mind.

- **Translating**—The act of connecting the mind actions to complex thinking processes, by using both terms together. *"By hypothesis I mean what might be the effects...?"*

- **Types of thinking**—Basic actions of the mind, or classifications of basic acts of thinking that are: **Recall**, **Cause and Effect**, **Similarity**, **Difference**, **Idea to Example**, **Example to Idea**, and **Evaluation**.

- **Typology**—A systematic classification according to general type; as in the ThinkTrix Typology.

- **Variety**—A subcategory of a kind of ThinkLink.

- **Wait Time**—The period of time between the teacher or student's question and the first person who responds. This interval should be at least 3 seconds. This is known as Wait Time I. Wait Time II is the time interval between the student's response and the response of the next speaker, teacher, or student. Wait Time, or Think Time, can only be achieved if hands are raised on a cue from the teacher or leader.

- **Weird facts**—Unusual, to the mind novel, facts, or phenomena. These cognitive incongruities, being previously unknown, stimulate a drive to know more, to confirm, or to contradict. They are essential to motivating inquiry in the classroom and are known in science as discrepant events.

Bibliography

The ThinkTrix Bibliography is a reminder that this metacognitive typology has been thoroughly field-tested.

Adger, Carolyn, Maya Kalyanpur, Dana Peterson, and Teresa Bridger. 1995. *Engaging Students: Thinking, Talking, Cooperating.* Thousand Oaks, CA: Corwin Press.

Arends, Richard I. 1997. *Classroom Instruction and Management.* McGraw-Hill. 224–226.

Beyer, Barry K. 1997. *Improving Student Thinking: A Comprehensive Approach.* Allyn & Bacon. 24–25.

Bridger, Teresa. 1996. *The use of "ThinkTrix" as a questioning strategy for teaching of high school students identified with learning disabilities.* **Doctoral Dissertation.** Fairfax, VA: George Mason University.

Bridger, Teresa. 1990. *A Scenario for the implementation of the question/response cues for special education students.* **Unpublished Paper.**

Carroll, Kathleen. 2007. *A Guide to Great Field Trips.* Chicago, IL: Zephyr Press. 122–127, 163–166, 175.

Carroll, Kathleen. 2000. *Science for Every Learner: Brain-Compatible Pathways to Scientific Literacy.* Tucson, AZ: Zephyr Press. **Introduction, xiii.**

Carter, Carol, Joyce Bishop, and Sarah Lyman Kravits. 1996. *Keys to Success: How to Achieve Your Goals. 2nd Ed.* Upper Saddle River, NJ: Prentice Hall. 124–128

Carter, Carol, Joyce Bishop, and Sarah Lyman Kravits. 2006. *Success Instructional Manual to Accompany Keys to Success.* Upper Saddle River, NJ: Pearson Education, Inc. 297–302.

Coley, Joan D. and Dianne M. Hoffman. 1990. *Overcoming learned helplessness in at-risk readers.* **Journal of Reading.** April, 497–502.

Coley, Joan D. and Thommie DePinto Piercy. 1988. *Merging reciprocal teaching question/response cues.* **Unpublished Paper.**

Coley, Joan D. and Thommie DePinto Piercy. 1989. *Reciprocal teaching: theme and variations.* **Unpublished Paper.**

Coley, Joan D., Sharon Craig, Thommie DePinto Piercy, and Rosalie Gardiner. 1993. *From college to classroom: Three teachers' accounts of their adaptations of reciprocal teaching.* **Elementary School Journal.** Chicago, IL: University of Chicago Press. Vol. 94, No. 2, 256–266.

Craig, Sharon, Thommie DePinto Piercy, Rosalie Gardiner, M. Marks, and M. Pressley. 1993. *Three teachers' adaptations of reciprocal teaching in comparison to traditional reciprocal teaching.* **Elementary School Journal.** Chicago, IL: University of Chicago Press. Vol. 94, No. 2, 267–283.

Critical Thinking Year Two. 1992–93. **Curriculum Guide.** Henrico City Public School System. Richmond, VA. 77–104.

DePinto Piercy, Thommie. 1986. *Listening to children's voices.* **Unpublished Paper.**

DePinto Piercy, Thommie. 1987. *The extension of thinking skills in comprehension.* **Unpublished Paper.**

(continued)

Bibliography (continued)

DePinto Piercy, Thommie. 1988. *Action Research: A teacher's perspective.* **Reading: Issues and Practices 5.**

DePinto Piercy, Thommie. 1997. *The effects of multi-strategy instruction as measured by a standardized assessment of reading comprehension.* **Doctoral Dissertation.** College Park, MD: University of Maryland.

English, Evelyn. 1999. *Gift of Literacy for the Multiple Intelligence Classroom.* Arlington Heights, IL: Skylight Publishers, Inc. 144–146.

Figler, Howard, Carol Carter, Joyce Bishop, and Sarah Lyman Kravits. 2002. *Keys to Liberal Arts Success.* Upper Saddle River, NJ: Pearson Education Inc. 118–135.

Forte, Imogene and Sandra Schurr. 1993. *The Definitive Middle School Guide.* Nashville, TN: Incentive Publications. 217, 218.

Foster, Karen K. 2006. *Spin the wheel of thinking to activate critical thought.* **IRA: Journal of Content Area Reading.** Vol. 5, No. 1. 67–79.

Hoffman, Barbara. 1987. *Thirty-four years later.* **The Early Adolescence Magazine.** 1(4), 6–9.

Keeling, Janet, Editor. 1993. *The Middle School Guide.* Incentive Publications, Inc. 24–25.

King, Alison. 1992. *Facilitating elaborative learning through guided student-generated questioning.* Educational Psychiatrist. Vol. 27, No. 1, 111–126.

Knight, Janice E. 1990. *Coding journal entries.* **Journal of Reading.** 34(1), 42–47.

Koza, Nancy. 1990. *A Scenario for the Implementation of ThinkTrix at the Primary Level.* **Unpublished Paper.**

Lyman, Frank T. and Shirley Rogers. 1996. *Building philosophical foundations: The ThinkTrix model in the classroom.* Bookbird. Vol. 34, No. 3. Fall.

Lyman, Frank T. 1998. *The Teaching of the Uses of the ThinkTrix.*

Lyman, Frank T. 1995. *Clarity and Cooperative Learning: The concrete-abstract connection.* **MAACIE Newsletter Nov./Dec. 1995.** MD: MAACIE Newsletter.

Lyman, Frank T. 1996. *Independent and cooperative interpretation of thinking prompts: learning to translate performance-based tasks through the ThinkTrix.* **MAACIE Newsletter Fall 1996.** MD: MAACIE Newsletter.

Lyman, Frank T. 1994. *Cooperative Learning and Every-Student-Response: Their Essential Relationship.* **MAACIE Newsletter, February 1994.** MD: MAACIE Newsletter. Vol. 7(3).

Lyman, Frank T., Nancy Koza, and Mary McKnight. 1993. *Every-Student-Response through transactional signaling: Cooperative cues for cooperative thinking* in **Cooperative Learning.** Cooperative Learning Press, CA: Vol. 13, No. 2.

Lyman, Frank T., Charlene Lopez, and Arlene Mindus. 2010. *The Shaping of Thought: ThinkLinks and Metacognition, A Teacher's Guide to Critical and Creative Thinking in Response to Literature.* NJ: Spotlight Learning, an imprint of PrintPod, Inc.

(continued)

Bibliography (continued)

Lyman, Frank T. 1998. *The Teaching of the Uses of the ThinkTrix,* in Carol Carter, Joyce Bishop, Sarah Lyman Kravits, and Kathleen Cole: *Adopter's Resource Kit for Keys to Success,* 2nd Ed. Upper Saddle River, NJ: Prentice Hall. 59–62.

Lyman, Frank T. 1987. *The ThinkTrix: A classroom tool for thinking in response to reading.* **Reading: Issues and Practices, Yearbook of the State of Maryland International Reading Association Council.** Vol. 4, 15–18.

Lyman, Frank T. 1992. *Think-Pair-Share, ThinkTrix, ThinkLinks, and Weird Facts: Interactive system for cooperative thinking.* **In Enhancing Thinking Through Cooperative Learning.** Edited by Neil Davidson and Toni Worsham. Columbia University, NY: Teachers College Press. 169–182.

Lyman, Frank T. 2005. *ThinkTrix,* the SmartCard. San Clemente, CA: Kagan Publishing.

McTighe, Jay and Frank T. Lyman. 1989. *Cueing Thinking in the Classroom: The Promise of Theory-embedded Tools.* Educational Leadership. April. Alexandria, VA: ASCD. 18–24.

McTighe, Jay and Frank T. Lyman. 1992. *Mind tools for matters of the mind in If Minds Matter, A Forward to the Future.* Vol. II. Edited by Costa, Arthur, James Bellanca, and Robin Fogerty. Palatine, IL: Skylight Publishing, Inc. 71–90.

Polack, Sam. 1989. *The continuum within each thinking type: The third dimension.* **Unpublished Paper.**

Ransom, Kathryn, Doris Roettger, and Phyllis Staplin, Project Coordinators. 1995. *Reading Assessment in Practice: Book of Readings & Video Tapes.* IRA. Appendix E.

Rogers, Shirley. 1990. *Applications and scenarios for the implementation of ThinkTrix in intermediate grades: Social studies/language arts.* **Unpublished Paper.**

Solomon, Richard and Elaine Solomon. 1995. *Handbook for the fourth R: Relationship Activities for Cooperative & Collegial learning.* Columbia, MD. **Chapters 6 & 7.**

Solomon, Richard and Elaine Solomon. 2009. *Toolbox for Teachers and Mentors: Moving Madrichim to Mentor Teachers and Beyond.* Tucson, AZ: Wheatmark Publishing. 73–79.

Stiggins, Richard, Judith Arter, Jan Chappuis, and Stephen Chappuis. 2005. *Classroom Assessment for Student Learning. Assessment Training Institute.* Portland, OR. 267–269.

Valencia, Sheila, E. Hiebert, and Peter Afflerbach. 1994. *User's Handbook. Authentic Reading Assessment Practices and Possibilities.* Newark, DE: IRA. Appendix E.

Winebrenner, Susan. 2014. *Teaching Kids with Learning Difficulties in the Regular Classroom.* Minneapolis, MN: Free Spirit Publishing, 3rd Ed. 69–70.

Winebrenner, Susan and Dina Brulles. 2008. *The Cluster Grouping Handbook: How to Challenge Gifted Students and Improve Achievement for All.* Minneapolis, MN: Free Spirit Publishing. 138–140.

Winebrenner, Susan and Dina Brulles. 2012. *Teaching Gifted Kids in Today's Classroom: Strategies and Techniques Every Teacher Can Use.* Minneapolis, MN: Free Spirit Publishing, 3rd Ed. 157–160.

Appreciations

To some of the educators who have been essential to the evolution of ThinkTrix

Ann Mintz, Monica Palumbo, and Molly Ketterer, who helped produce the IRA video of ThinkTrix in action.

Arlene Mindus and Charlene Lopez, who were co-discoverers of the ThinkTrix typology (sculptors of the pattern in the stone).

Belinda Miller, who invented the two-sided ThinkTrix and made the game changing video of her two "Belinda's Boys."

Jay McTique, who arranged comprehensive videotaping of ThinkTrix in action.

Hema Kumar, who made ThinkTrix central to her first-grade classroom.

Jeanne Dussault and Thommie DePinto Piercy, who made ThinkTrix central to graduate coursework, and inspired action research and publications.

Kim Flyr, whose demonstrations of ThinkTrix in first grade, made an impact on urban educators.

Laura "Chips" Merkle, who did extraordinary work with language disability students using ThinkLinks, Think-Pair-Share, and ThinkTrix.

Nancy Koza, who made ThinkTrix integral to her first grade, instituted hand signals, and contributed significantly to this book's content.

Neil Davidson, who shows the video *Belinda's Boys* and advocates ThinkTrix with cooperative learning.

Sam Polack, who developed the concept of a complexity dimension to ThinkTrix.

Sarah Lyman Kravits, who coined the term "mind actions," and included the ThinkTrix strategy in her college textbook.

Sharon Vargo Olson, who designed the first ThinkTrix grids.

Shirley Rogers, who made and makes ThinkTrix central to several classrooms, at all performance levels, in varied settings and in several grades.

Suzanne Levin-Weinberg, who researched and first brought ThinkTrix to mathematics in secondary-teacher education.

Tamera Sherr, who brought ThinkTrix to her urban fifth-grade classroom with great success.

Teresa Bridger, who brought ThinkTrix to special education students, cowrote a book featuring ThinkTrix, and wrote a doctoral dissertation on ThinkTrix.

Thomas Payne, who coined the term "ThinkTrix."

Richard Solomon, who brings ThinkTrix to Jewish Education.

Thommie DePinto Piercy, who, with her fifth-grade teammates, combined ThinkTrix with ThinkLinks to create a total metacognitive classroom(s), modeling for teachers around Maryland.

Tom Bruner, whose fifth-grade students did the first labeling of ThinkLinks according to thinking type, which led the way to ThinkTrix, and who coined the term "ThinkLinks."

Tom Cole, who first used the ThinkTrix grid with individual students.

A Note to Teachers and Students

ThinkTrix strategy and tools, and ThinkLinks are all inventions of teachers and students. Anyone using this book should realize that the inventing has not stopped. Ongoing innovation and spin-offs that you provide will further evolve the strategy to the point where it represents a paradigm shift in learning how to think. With your work, ThinkTrix will become a "theory of everything," that on a practical level will eclipse all other typologies and "lists" in helping to shift the "actions"—the "mind's activity"—to students.

Notes

ThinkTrix: Tools to Teach 7 Essential Thinking Skills
Kagan Publishing • (800) 933-2667 • www.KaganOnline.com

Notes

Notes

Notes

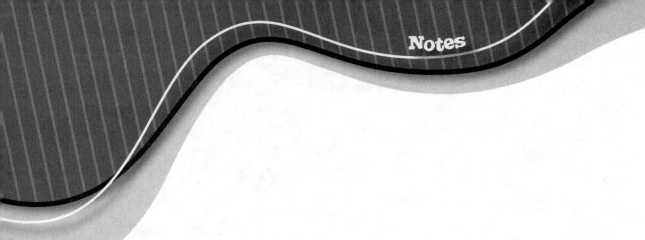

ThinkTrix: Tools to Teach 7 Essential Thinking Skills
Kagan Publishing • (800) 933-2667 • www.KaganOnline.com